FASHION MAGIC

FUN WAYS TO TRANSFORM YOUR CLOTHES

MICHELLE HUBERMAN

PIATKUS

© 1989 Michelle Huberman

First published in 1989 by
Judy Piatkus (Publishers) Limited,
5 Windmill Street, London W1P 1HF

British Library Cataloguing in Publication Data

Huberman, Michelle
  Fashion magic.
  1. Women's clothing – Manuals
  I. Title
  646′.34

  ISBN 0–86188–884–7

Edited by Susan Fleming
Designed by Dave Allen
Photographs by Ron Sutherland
Hair and make-up by Frances Prescott

Phototypeset in 10/11 Linotron Times by
Phoenix Photosetting, Chatham, Kent
Printed and bound in Spain by
Mateu Cromo S.A., Pinto, Madrid

This book is dedicated to my wonderful mother, Thelma Huberman,
and my late grandpa, Aubrey Segal.

Contents

Acknowledgements

Producing *Fashion Magic* with Piatkus Books has been an exciting experience. I am grateful to the endless dedication and energies of Gill Cormode and Susan Mears. As I am one of those people who talk incessantly with their hands, I am indebted to my editor, Susan Fleming, for translating my sign language and enthusiasm into understandable text.

I would like to thank my family and friends, customers and suppliers who have helped me along in my career. Without their support I would never have achieved so much.

Special thanks to my business partners David Morgan and Harold Karmel, and to all my staff who have continued superbly during my frequent absences while producing this book. *Merci beaucoup* to Zina Kheloufi, who was my pillar of strength in Paris.

Lastly thank you to Jonathan Hertz, who has motivated, encouraged and supported me throughout.

The author and publishers wish to thank the following models who have appeared in the book: Alexandra, Annabelle, Annamie, Carolyn, Clare, Clarissa, Helen, Nse, Raphael, Rebecca, Sally, Sophie, Vicki and Wei San.

Introduction

If you've ever looked in your wardrobe and thought you had nothing to wear, think again. If you've ever thought you couldn't afford clothes in the latest fashion trend, once more think again. For *Fashion Magic* is an introduction to a host of ways in which you can transform garments, new or old, into something exciting, innovative and fashionable.

I first became interested in decorating my clothes when, as a teenager, I kept having to wear clothes handed down on from my older sisters. I was determined to make them look different – and succeeded. Later, when I went to work for a fashion-accessory manufacturer, I was in seventh heaven, surrounded by trimmings, fabrics, studs, feathers, beads and sequins. Any leftovers soon found their way on to my clothes. Gradually I started to do similar things for friends, followed by paying clients, then it grew until I was running a spectacularly successful small factory in Paris, the centre of the fashion world. (I saw my ideas adorning film stars in the south of France, and several European royals.) I now have a factory in London, which is inundated with orders and I am teaching people to start their own garment decorating businesses. And it all stemmed from a resentment of hand-me-downs. . .

You don't need to be particularly artistic to be able to work fashion magic on your clothes – though a good eye helps. You don't even need to be able to sew, as many of the decorations are painted, glued, clamped, or machine sewn on. All the ideas can be achieved in a very short time too, important if you want virtually instant transformation and are impatient like me. And the materials to use are not very expensive to buy, vital if you're on a budget.

One rule I would pass on is that if you see something you like, *buy* it or *acquire* it. Become like a magpie, and collect everything and anything and keep your trimmings in colour-coded boxes. The more variety there is in your collection – of sequin motifs, braids, beads, buttons etc – the more choice you will have the next time you want to decorate something. I'm always on the look-out for my trimmings, visiting haberdashery shops and old clothes stalls, and traipsing around hardware shops for feather dusters (an excellent source of feathers) and to the local shoemaker for leather scraps. I hope this book will encourage the Aladdin's cave world of haberdashery shops to expand their ranges even further. *Think* decoration too, and before throwing out a garment because it's too old-fashioned or tatty, consider whether there's anything on it, like buttons, that could be saved. Keep broken jewellery too; those lovely ornaments can be stuck on a sweater. Use your decorative eye too when shopping – that T-shirt may be plain and boring, but imagine what you could do to it!

So, you have a pair of pink jeans and nothing to go with them: decorate a white T-shirt with paint, sequins, polyester flowers or a transfer print in the same pink. An instant outfit. You have a stain on the shoulder of a beloved dress (why is it that parties seem inevitably to mean red wine shoulder stains?): cover it up with a bit of fashion magic in the form of a cascade of flowers, a design of leather pieces, a sequin motif or a spray of feathers. (Make earrings or a hairpiece to match the decoration, and that dress will have a completely new life.) A sweater bought cheaply from a chainstore looks a bit boring: with a few lengths of sequin braid, a couple of motifs and some judicious cutting, tucking and sewing, you can have something that is quite unique and that would cost you a fortune in an exclusive knitwear shop.

Admiration is a great motivator when you're just starting. It gives you the confidence to go on to greater things. Nothing beats that smug feeling when a friend asks where you got that super outfit from, and you can reply, 'I made it myself'. I love having people around me when I work. It always helps to have someone to say, 'Yes, that looks terrific' or 'It's too much, take off a couple of flowers.' The best model for your creations is always yourself. Try the plain garment on before transforming it, then pin the trimmings in position. You'll find that what looks good on the table can look a disaster on the body! If the tassels or dangly bits are in the wrong place you could end up looking like a Turkish belly dancer!!

I have divided the book up into sections which give you ideas of how to use glitter, leather, flowers, feathers, zips (yes, zips!), buttons, bows, paints and glues. There are detailed instructions attached to some of the 'recipes', and more basic techniques at the back of the book. I would urge you to read carefully through each set of instructions before you start, just to see what's involved – timings, for instance, which are given for a fairly experienced worker and may take a little longer to do until you get the knack of the various basic techniques. However, having said that, I don't think it's important to follow the instructions to the letter. The ideas in the text and in the photographs are there to inspire you, to get your own imagination working. I hope this book will inspire everyone to see their clothes as a canvas. Please adopt, adapt, and improve, and I wish you success and fun with your own brand of fashion magic!

Michelle Huberman

Michelle Huberman,
March 1989

All That Glitters

Adding sparkle to clothes is easy and fun. A few sequins and studs can transform a shirt or sweater in minutes. Dazzle your friends with your 'designer' style.

Just like a magpie, you have to collect anything and everything glittery that you see and like. In haberdashery departments you'll find all sizes and colours of studs, sequins, pearls and diamantés – loose, iron-on, clawed, ropes, etc. Always buy more than you need because extras can be used on hair clips, bags, belts or jewellery. In the same places you'll also find sequin and stone motifs and beaded nets and laces that will deceive your friends into thinking you've spent hours making them (but all the hard work has already been done for you in the Far East). If you are going to use these motifs, however, don't just plonk them on by themselves: make them individual to you by adding braids, diamantés, feathers, tassels, etc. You'll see a few ideas in the following pages.

Another possible source of supply is junk shops or jumble sales. Often you can see boxes of motifs, beads or buttons on sale for just a few pence. An old evening dress might be well past its best, but it may have some feature like a waistband, shoulder detail or beading just waiting to be used. It's worth spending the money on the dress to unpick and keep them.

If a dress or shirt you own is worn out, remove any zips, buttons or motifs that can be re-used. This way you should soon build up a glittery collection second to none.

Sparkle T-shirts

These fun styles are very quick and easy to make and can be adapted to any style of T-shirt. Try the same idea on a fine-knit sweater as well!

Pink T-shirt

You can buy T-shirts with already-printed faces or you can print one on yourself (see page 89) and jazz it up.

Time: *about 30 minutes*

Cleaning: *hand wash inside out, do not iron transfer or decorations*

To decorate:

about 12 iron-on crystal diamantés

gold glitter plastic-look fabric paint

2 large blue diamantés

gold sequin motif with tassel

pair of false eyelashes

gold sequin rope

*gold and turquoise lurex yarn
  (used for crocheting)*

1 ribbon bow

black sequin rope

Tools and equipment:

iron

paintbrush

METHOD

1 Place the crystal diamantés randomly over the front of the T-shirt around the face and iron on (see page 116).

2 Using the gold glitter fabric paint, put large blobs over the eyes, and stick on the two large blue diamantés for the pupils. Also glue on the sequin motif with tassel for an earring.

3 Using a little more glitter paint, stick on the false eyelashes around the eyes. When the glue has dried, trim them to look more 'natural'.

4 To highlight the hair – here a major part of the design – take the gold glitter paint (or any colour you like) and run the tip of the squeezy bottle along the strands of the hair.

5 Then, using the gold sequin rope and the two colours of yarn, glue them along lines of the hair too, to look like curls.

6 To 'make up' the face, I've used some gold fabric paint as eye shadow and blusher. Just squeeze a little out, then use a brush to smooth it over the areas. The glue in the paint dries transparent, and you just see the glitter.

7 Make a ribbon bow and stick in place in the hair with a large blob of fabric paint.

8 Finally, to give the effect of a dress, I outlined a little *bustier* shape with fabric paint and then stuck on a length of black sequin braid. I pulled off a few individual sequins from the end of the strip and stuck them on individual little blobs of fabric paint. (This comes through the holes in the sequin, and dries to look exactly like the beads used in hand-sewn sequins.)

9 Leave the T-shirt to dry for 4 hours.

Diamanté cat's eyes for the Turquoise T-shirt.

Turquoise T-shirt

The foiled pattern of a cat on this T-shirt was very flat, so I thought a more three-dimensional approach would lift it. The dangling bell is a real cat's bell, bought from a pet shop. Lots of T-shirts can be bought with an animal face already on them – or, of course, you can transfer one on (see page 122). I've marbled gold and silver foils together here. Adapt the ideas below for a dog, tiger, lion, etc.

Time: *about 1 hour*

Cleaning: *hand wash inside out, do not iron transfer or decorations*

To decorate:

2 large green diamantés

green and clear glitter plastic-look fabric paints

loose blue-black sequins

gold moulded pearl rope

red iron-on diamantés

a length of ribbon or braid

1 small bell

about 12 studs

Tools and equipment:

iron

studding clamp

METHOD

1 Stick the large green diamantés on to the eyes using the green glitter paint in generous blobs. Straightaway this relieves the flatness of the design, and the diamantés catch the light well.

2 For the nose, cover it with a thin layer of the clear paint, and pile on the blue-black sequins, very close together, to create that massed effect.

3 Use the moulded pearl rope for the whiskers. Measure each whisker carefully and sew them on close together at the nose end. Then arrange in different directions and attach each by sewing on a few centimetres from the end.

4 Create a tongue shape, or cover the tongue already there, by massing red iron-on diamantés together. Cover with paper and iron on as described on page 116.

5 Cats wear collars and bells, so cut a fairly generous length of ribbon (or braid), and thread on a little bell. Stud the ribbon at regular intervals (see page 118) and then attach each folded-over end to the T-shirt with a stud.

6 To finish off the collar of the T-shirt, I've ironed on some crystal diamantés at regular intervals.

Detail showing a polyester butterfly with diamanté antennae.

White T-shirt

I always think abstract designs are easier to achieve than symmetrical. A star can go very wrong, for instance, but if you make a mistake with an abstract design it won't show and it won't matter!

Time: *30 minutes*

Cleaning: *hand wash inside out, do not iron, dry flat*

To decorate:
fabric paints in pink and turquoise
a selection of diamantés and pearls (sew-on and iron-on) in crystal, pink and turquoise
2 sequin butterfly motifs
2 larger polyester butterflies
moulded pearl rope
2 larger diamantés, pearls or beads

Tools and equipment:
iron
needles and thread
pins
Copydex glue

METHOD

1 Put a piece of greaseproof paper between the T-shirt layers, then, using the fabric paints, I put some squiggles around the top part of the T-shirt in pink and turquoise. To seal and dry quickly, cover with another sheet of greaseproof paper and iron.

2 Then, scattered randomly, attach a selection of the diamantés and pearls – some can be inside the coloured blotches, some directly on to the white fabric. Decorate the collar of the T-shirt with equally spaced iron-on crystal diamantés (see page 116).

3 Before attaching the sequin butterflies, decorate them with four pink pearls as markings (sew or iron-on).

4 Next, to establish the position of the four butterflies and pearl rope, try the T-shirt on. This is vital, or you might end up looking like a go-go dancer with a butterfly in a very inappropriate place! Pin all four butterflies where you want them, and position the lengths of pearl rope.

5 Sew on the ends of the pearl rope then attach the two larger butterflies, using clawed larger diamantés, or sewn-on beads or pearls. Attach a few diamantés to the T-shirt fabric to look like antennae.

6 Add some tiny lengths of moulded pearl rope – approximately 15 cm (6 inches) – as antennae for the sequin butterflies. Bend in half and stitch along two or three pearls as close as possible to the right end of the butterfly. Sew or glue the sequin butterflies on at the shoulders.

Shirts with a Shimmer

Try some of these ideas on old shirts you would otherwise throw away and add something special to your wardrobe. I love the idea of sparkle on denim or chambray – it glamorizes traditional working clothes. The following two shirts demonstrate this versatile approach.

Washed-out Black Denim Shirt

This ordinary shirt has been quite radically transformed by simple diamantés and studs. Team it with a stunning belt for a dramatic look.

Time: *60 minutes*

Cleaning: *hand wash*

To decorate:

at least 150 crystal diamantés

at least 100 silver claw studs

Tools and equipment:

stud clamp

measuring tape or ruler

METHOD

1 Try your shirt on first to see where it could be highlighted – the collar, pockets, yoke, sleeves, front, back, etc. It all depends on the style, but don't ever *over*-do it. Here I chose to decorate the front edges of the collar, the shoulder seams, tops of the pockets, cuffs and the front opening.

2 Start off with the studs, clamping them in your chosen places about 2.5 cm (1 inch) apart (see page 118). They must be even, so measure carefully with a tape or ruler. For symmetry, start at the top of the button section (match both sides carefully); on the points of the collar; in the middle of the pocket line; at the shoulder line.

3 In between the studs, iron, sew or clamp on diamantés (here they're clawed, see page 116). This is easier as you can judge position and distance with your eyes.

You can always try the same idea on a pair of jeans. This idea works best if you follow the line of the seams. It accentuates the cut of shirts or trousers and brings the garment to life. For a change, use alternate diamanté colours, and try mixing gold and silver studs – that way you don't have to be tied to one or other colour for your jewellery.

> **Tip** It's well-nigh impossible to specify how many studs, diamantés, etc you'll need for a project like this. It all depends on the style of the shirt you buy, and you may need more or less. However, it's always best, I think, to buy *more* than you need because you might break some, or the claws might not go in properly. You might also want to repeat the pattern on your jeans or skirt too.

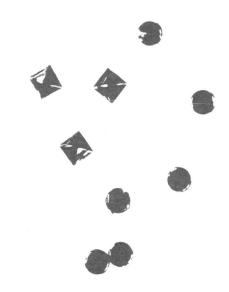

Beaded Net Chambray Shirt

Chambray shirts are popular and look good – but they can look *even better*!

Time: *about 40 minutes*

Cleaning: *hand wash, do not iron net*

To decorate:

measured length of beaded net (see below)

measured length of crystal-stoned braid (see below)

20–30 crystal iron-on diamantés

Tools and equipment:

measuring tape

pins

sewing machine – size 120 needles

transparent and polyester all-purpose threads

scissors

iron

METHOD

1 First of all, measure all round the yoke of the shirt, front and back, to ascertain the basic length of beaded net you need – then buy *double* that length. Measure where you want to add braid – for example, around the yoke on top of the lace, round the collar, the cuffs, or the pocket tops of jeans or skirt. Buy a little extra just in case – it won't ever be wasted.

2 Take the length of net and either gather it slightly by hand or by machine. If you have a machine use the largest stitch and loosen the tension.

3 Place the slightly gathered lace around the yoke, starting at the front opening (but not covering the buttons, see page 114). Pin at each end – right side to right side, the frill *upwards* towards the collar. Ease the net to fit around the yoke line, tightening the gathers to help fit, and leaving more gathers where the bends are.

4 Stitch along to the seam line – by hand or by machine – and then trim the raw edges (they won't fray). Fold the frill *down*, towards the bottom of the shirt, to cover all the edges.

5 Lie the crystal-stoned braid along the top of the net fold on the seam line, starting at the same starting point, and pin in place. Do the same on the collar (and wherever else you want to have the braid).

6 Sew by hand using an overlocking stitch and transparent thread. If using the machine, sew on as described on page 113, using the zigzag so that the needle goes into the Chambray on one side, the net on the other. Take it very slowly to ensure that the needle does not hit the diamantés.

7 For the collar, start the braid at the top under the chin. When you come to the points you'll have to partially snip the braid, as it won't turn on a severe angle like this.

8 As a final decorative touch, scatter some crystal diamantés around the yoke, front and back. This should be quite geometrical on this shirt because of the style, and also because of the braid which is very definite and regular.

Tip When repeating a design on shirt and jeans, don't make it too symmetrical. Have the matching motifs on *opposite* sides.

Also, if you want to decorate the back of jeans with glitter, only do so on the top of the pockets or above: if you have diamantés or sequins too low down, you'll break them when you sit down – and it wouldn't be all that comfortable either!

Child's Shirt and Jeans

Although this idea is shown here as a child's outfit, it is easily adaptable for adults – and in fact it's been one of my best-selling designs. It started off as a means of using up lots of bits and pieces, and at one time was so popular that I had almost every concierge in Paris sewing frantically to fulfil the orders! (I've seen this outfit on a couple of famous film stars!)

Time: *50 minutes*

Cleaning: *hand wash or dry clean* (**F**) *do not iron trimmings*

To decorate:

9 small pastel-coloured sequin motifs

moulded pearl rope in pink and white

assorted pearls, sequins and diamantés

Tools and equipment:

pins

sewing machine (optional)

needles and thread

METHOD

1 Choose materials which are all basically in the same pastel colour scheme. Taking a selection of small motifs (you could use more for adult clothes), I've scattered them where I thought they looked best on the skirt when tried on – a pink butterfly on the right shoulder, a bunch of balloons on the pocket, and a small bird complete with hanging pearl beside the buttons on the left-hand side. Place where you want on the jeans, then pin them and sew (see page 115).

2 For the shirt shoulder detail and the jeans pocket detail, I've used four identical motifs that look like bunches of grapes. One is on the left-hand dropped shoulder seam of the shirt, one on the pocket; they're both on the *opposite*, right-hand pocket of the jeans. Pin and sew them in place.

3 To add another dimension, I've looped between both sets of matching motifs two lengths of moulded pearl rope in the same colour. You'll have to measure this on the child or yourself; roughly speaking, measure the space between the motifs, double it, and add an extra 20 cm (8 inches).

4 Catch the two ends together at one end and stitch them down at the top of the design. Put the two ropes together on the other motif and let them hang naturally, one slightly longer than the other, before cutting. Sew them on together as above. They should look as if they were branches leading to the grape bunch. Cut small lengths of pearl rope and sew on as antennae for the sequinned butterflies.

5 I've scattered some pearls on at random, about five on each side of the shirt and jeans (and of course you could decorate the back of the shirt as well). In between these I've attached other sequin shapes – little stars and flowers – with a bead in the middle.

6 On the shirt shoulder seams I've added some evenly spaced diamantés, and a little trio of crystal diamantés on each collar point.

Pocket detail.

Party Stunners

The bases for these bustiers are strapless long-line bras from the lingerie department of a national chainstore. Buy these new for this idea to work successfully. (By the way, both the leather jackets were made by me – but they're rather beyond the scope of this book!)

Black Bustier

Time: *about 25 minutes*

Cleaning: *hand wash, do not iron*

To decorate:

about 1 m (a good yard) black iridescent sequin rope

black iridescent diamantés

black iridescent sequin and stone motif

Tools and equipment:

pins

sewing machine (optional)

transparent and black all-purpose polyester threads

METHOD

1 The black bra had a little bow in the front which I cut off. The back was elasticated so could not be sequined. So I pinned the sequin rope around the front contours only, starting at the side seam.

2 Sew the rope on, by machine or hand (see page 112 for detailed instructions). Always follow the direction of the sequins if machining, otherwise it will catch. Finish off the ends neatly.

3 On each little curve of the top edge of the bra, add a little black diamanté (see page 116 and don't forget to place greaseproof paper underneath and on top).

4 Pin the motif in the centre of the bra, the top overlapping the sequin rope, and sew on. This ties the whole design together.

White Bustier

Time: *about 25 minutes*

Cleaning: *hand wash, do not iron*

To decorate:

iron-on crystal diamantés

Tools and equipment:

iron

METHOD

1 The decoration here is simplicity itself, and you can use any pattern you want. The first thing to do, as always, is to try the bra on to see where the design will be most appropriate.

2 The top of the cups and the front panel were where I decided the diamantés would look best. I worked out the design, arranging loose diamantés on the fabric, then ironed them on (see page 116) when I was satisfied with the layout.

Choose a motif that will match the sequin rope and diamantés.

Evening Elegance

Evening is generally considered the best time for glittering extravaganza, and the following three ideas should certainly inspire you.

Khaki Tassel Sweater

A simple raglan sweater can be made to look really special with the addition of studs and tassels – but do be careful with your colour combinations. The khaki and gold here are subtle, I think, and that's the effect you want.

Time: *about 1½ hours*

Cleaning: *hand wash or dry clean*

To decorate:

about 250 studs
14 small tassels

Tools and equipment:

pins
iron-on interfacing
iron
ruler or measuring tape
tailor's chalk
stud clamping tool
embroidery needle

METHOD

1 First of all, try the sweater on and decide where exactly you want the studs. Make sure you've got the shoulder pads in, so that the sweater sits correctly and you can judge where the design should begin and end – on the end of the shoulder and at the front, for instance. Put pins at these points.

2 To reinforce the fabric at the neckline, so that the studs stay in nicely, arrange interfacing over the areas you want to cover. Use one that is made for knitted fabrics, so that the sweater will still have some stretch in it. Cut it to fit your projected design and then iron in place onto the reverse.

3 Now mark your design on the shoulders of the sweater using the ruler or measuring tape and the tailor's chalk. I used the raglan seams as a guide (a central shoulder seam could also be a starting point), and marked out little dots at 2 cm (¾ inch) intervals along the seams, and then in sprays out from that seam at the same 2 cm (¾ inch) intervals. There are ten sprays going out on either shoulder, 2 cm (¾ inch) apart.

4 Match the shoulders carefully and then put the studs in, pushing carefully through knit and interfacing, and folding the prongs over with the clamp (see page 118).

5 Then, to make the central front and back designs, I measured from the centre, and marked dots with tailor's chalk at the same 2 cm (¾ inch) intervals. Insert studs.

6 I've also studded the cuffs, but interfacing cannot be used here as cuffs are too stretchy. There's not really enough thickness for the studs to hold correctly, so be very careful when clamping them shut. Use the ribbing as a guide, trying to keep to the same measures as above.

7 To finish the sweater off and make it look even more special, I've hung a small gold tassel from each point – that same 2 cm (¾ inch) below the bottom stud. There are five on the front and back, one on each shoulder, and one on the outside of each cuff. Bought tassels usually have two threads at the top with which to attach them. They can easily be threaded onto an embroidery needle and 'sewn on'.

Red Sweater with Cut Sleeves

This was a very plain, classic, round-necked sweater which, with a little ingenuity, artistry and decoration, has been transformed into something very special. You should practise the lettuce-leaf effect (see page 113) on old sweaters or T-shirts first – any fabric that is close machine-knitted – using cheap braid the same width as the sequin braid.

Time: *about 1½ hours*

Cleaning: *hand wash, do not iron trimmings*

To decorate:

lots of sequin braid (at least twice or even three times the measured length

about 8–10 black sequin motifs (depending on size)

Tools and equipment:

sewing machine

transparent and polyester all-purpose threads

small sharp scissors and shears

pins

interfacing

iron

black fabric paint pen

METHOD

1 First of all, cut the arms – for which you've got to have loads of confidence! (Practise on old sweaters first, *not* on a new expensive one!) Lie the sweater flat, with the seams of the sleeves straight, and measure down about 5 cm (2 inches) from each shoulder seam. Cut in with little scissors first, then use large shears to cut bodly straight down the outside fold of the sleeve to the cuff.

2 Then turn to page 113 for a more detailed explanation of how to achieve the ruffled, lettuce-leaf effect. Starting at the top or bottom of the cut on the sleeve, place the knit on the left side and the sequin braid running through on the right side. Place the braid so that it only half overlaps on to the edge of the knit.

3 Start to sew, pulling the knit and releasing it when you've sewn as far as you can go, then pulling and releasing again. You're sewing the sequin braid on to the stretched fabric which, when it comes back to its normal tension, ruffles up.

4 Once you've done the first sleeve, finish off carefully by overlapping, and pulling off loose sequins at the end. The zigzag stitch sewing the braid on should seal the cut knit of the fabric, but do check afterwards just in case. If you've missed a bit here and there, just catch it and sew in by hand.

5 Do the second sleeve similarly, and then the cuffs, starting and ending on the seam. Finish off as above. Incidentally, the slash effect can also be attractive if kept to a shorter slash on the upper arm, or, if the full-length slash is joined together by a couple of stitches at the elbow.

6 Try the sweater on and pin the motifs carefully around the neck, but *below* the existing neckline. They must all touch or join if you want to achieve that continuous, chain-like effect.

7 Cut some interfacing to go around the shape where the top edges of the motifs fall, and iron into place from the reverse.

8 Remove sweater and machine sew the motifs on to the knit, around the edges as on page 115.

9 Then, taking the small, very sharp scissors, cut into the knit and the interfacing around the top edges of the motifs. You need to do this very carefully as there are so many little leaf edges, nooks and crannies.

10 The interfacing will stop the knit fabric running, but there may still be a few red edges showing. If so, run over them with the black fabric paint pen, then briefly iron to seal.

Cross-over Sweater

This sweater was bought in a chainstore, but with some inexpensive additions and trimmings you will have a garment that could easily sell for a fortune!

Time: *about 1 hour*

Cleaning: *hand wash, dry flat*

To decorate:

2 matching sequin motifs with tassels

length of pleated satin braid

length of beaded net

moulded pearl rope

Tools and equipment:

pins

sewing machine

transparent and polyester all-purpose threads

METHOD

1 First of all, try the sweater on and look at yourself in the mirror. Hold the motifs and braids in position and roughly pin them where you think they look best.

2 Start by doing the satin braid side of the cross-over. Lie the sweater flat, and re-pin the braid neatly on the fabric from the armhole to the waistband ribbing, as in the drawing. Cut the braid, allowing 5 cm (2 inches) over at each end to tuck under.

3 Pin one sequin motif over the top end of the satin braid, and sew in position (see page 115), using a large zigzag stitch.

4 Then, changing the stitch to a smaller zigzag, sew on the satin braid, attaching the moulded pearl rope at the same time (see page 113). Stitch down the turned-under bottom end of the braid.

5 On the other half of the cross-over, pin the beaded net in position (see page 114) on the inner edge of the welt, or ribbing. Sew on.

6 Pin the second sequin motif over the top raw edge of the lace and sew on as before. (I've turned this motif upside down and removed the tassel as I don't like things *too* symmetrical).

7 Finally, using more moulded pearl rope, I've created a lettuce-leaf effect (see page 113) round the as yet undecorated part of the neckline, from where the satin braid curves away round the back of the neck to the bottom of the net-decorated underside of the cross-over.

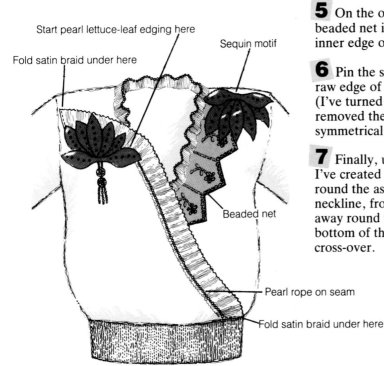

Start pearl lettuce-leaf edging here

Sequin motif

Fold satin braid under here

Beaded net

Pearl rope on seam

Fold satin braid under here

Guide to decorating cross-over sweater.

Skin Deep

Furriers and leather manufacturers (both fashion and furnishing) are the major sources of the scraps and remnants you will want. They can't use the bits left over from cutting out patterns, whether of fashion garments or leather sofas, but *you* can!

Encourage a friendly leather man near you, but be subtle. If you say you're making things for yourself, you might get scraps for next to nothing; if you admit you're making sweaters to sell for a fortune, you'll be charged considerably more! Chamois leather is available from a much more mundane source – the local garage or ironmongers. Gather bits and pieces in a multitude of colours, textures and finishes and you'll find a use for all of them at some time or another.

Many leathers can be adapted to create certain looks. You can spray-paint some, depending on their finishes (see page 121). You can also scrunch leather to get a chunkier, three-dimensional look (see page 39). Leather can be decorated, too, most simply with pinking shears, cut petal holes (see page 123) and studs (see page 118). It also responds well to glues. I find Copydex the best to use.

Sewing leather, however, requires some care. If you have a sewing machine, you'll need to use the strongest needles (120). Also, don't have the stitch holes too close together as leather tears easily.

A leather foot is useful, too, but if you don't have one you can improvise to prevent the leather slipping. Stick fabric sticking plaster over the bottom of the machine foot, and cut it to the shape of the foot with a Stanley knife or scalpel. Leave the hole for the needle free! Special leather needles are available for hand sewing.

If you have scruples about using animal skin, many of the effects in the following pages can be reproduced using imitations.

Smart Looks

Leather makes anything look expensive, but these looks are very simple and cheap to achieve as I've used leather scraps and remnants. The following four sweaters are smart enough to take you from the office to an evening cocktail party.

Zebra-patterned Sweatshirt

I've decorated this plain, classic sweatshirt with a zebra skin design using white leather on the black (you could use black leather on white).

Look at the patterns of the markings on a zebra to get the right effect. You could also create a tiger pattern using black and yellow. Actually *any* colour with black looks tigerish. Animal markings are a good source of inspiration, and they never go out of fashion.

Time: *60 minutes*

Cleaning: *dry clean* (F)

To decorate:

lots of long leather scraps

silver sequin braid (at least 10 m/11 yards)

Tools and equipment:

scissors

pins

sewing machine

glue gun with tape

transparent and polyester all-purpose threads

Tip If you can't get leather or leather imitation fabric, use any interwoven fabric. You'll have to use Bondaweb (see page 119) so that the fabric doesn't fray.

METHOD

1 All my leather pieces were acquired from a leather fashion house, and most were discarded hems. Cut them into jaggedy shapes, making each long piece come to a point. It's a completely random pattern.

2 With the sweater flat, arrange the pieces all over the right front of the sweater, up over the right shoulder, and all over the right sleeve. To keep them in position, turn up the edges of the pieces, run along the edges with the glue gun, and stick down flat.

3 Sew the sequin braid to the outside of the leather pieces (see page 112), with the centre hole of the sequins just on the edge of the leather. Use your largest and widest zigzag and go round every little slash, point, and squiggle. (I don't think this should be attempted by hand sewers . . .)

Tassel Earring

Buy or make a tassel earring (see page 123). Slot the loop over a sleeper earring, or attach to a clip. It's easy – and effective!

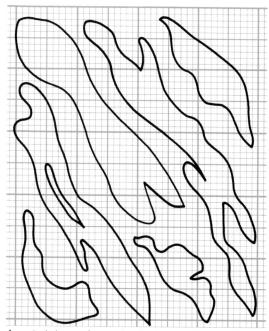

Assorted shapes for a zebra look.

White Sweater with Leaves and Roses

This white cotton sweater was bought incredibly cheaply in a street market – it must have been the bargain of the year. What I've done is decorate it with lots of toning gold, bronze and silver pieces of leather, cut into roses and leaves.

Time: *about 1½ hours*

Cleaning: *dry clean*

To decorate:

lots of toning pieces of metallic-coloured leather

gold and silver crochet yarn

gold and silver plastic-look fabric paints

about 10 gold beads

Tools and equipment:

Copydex glue

pair of rubber gloves

scissors and pinking shears

glue gun with repositioning glue or pins

sewing machine and leather foot

transparent and polyester all-purpose threads

METHOD

1 The design has seven scrunched leather circular 'roses' on it, and ten ordinary leather leaves, all of varying sizes. So the first thing is to scrunch up pieces of leather for the flowers, using the Copydex glue (and wearing your rubber gloves) as described on page 39.

2 When the scrunched pieces have dried, ease them out a little and cut them into circles of varying sizes with the pinking shears. Use the pinking shears to cut leaves of various sizes out of the remaining, non-scrunched, leather: some are long and thin, some are stubbier, and ideal for cutting little petal shapes out of to show the colour of the knitwear below (see page 123). From scraps lying around, I cut four little pieces of fringing (see page 44).

3 Try the sweater on, and use the glue gun or pins to position everything until you're pleased with the effect.

4 Then machine-sew in place, using a heavy needle and the leather foot. Use a straight stitch along the centre of the leaves, curving them slightly as you go, and leave the sides free. Sew around the edges of the circular roses, and don't forget to tuck in and catch the solid end of the little pieces of fringing when you sew them in place.

5 I've then used the gold and silver crochet yarns together to overlock the collar evenly. Use the rib as a spacing guide.

6 I've also overlocked the cuffs similarly. They were quite wide, so I turned them under twice, before overlocking – rather loosely, to keep the stretch of the cuff.

7 To give a bit more oomph and depth, I've done a few little branching squiggles with the gold and silver plastic-look fabric paints. Leave to dry thoroughly.

8 As a final touch, I threaded beads on to the ends of the fringing. The leather should hold them in place.

> **Tip** Many leathers can be hand-washed – with care, of course – but those which are 'foiled', as here, must be dry cleaned.

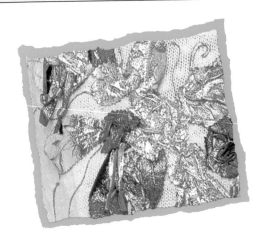

Detail of the rose and leaf design.

Leather-shouldered Sweater

The 'scrunching' technique is a wonderful way of using up any small but matching scraps of leather you have lying around. The layers are stuck together with glue, giving it a quite unique three-dimensional look. It's difficult to estimate how much leather you'll need – at least 60 cm (2 feet), I would guess. The idea works on T-shirts as well. You can create this painted leather look yourself (see page 121).

Time: *90 minutes*

Cleaning: *dry clean*

To decorate:

*lots of leather pieces (all sizes, best about 25 cm/
10 inches in diameter)*

about 400 studs

beaded fringing

Tools and equipment:

Copydex glue

pair of rubber gloves

studding clamp

Detail showing the three-dimensional leather shoulder decoration, studs and fringing.

METHOD

1 To scrunch the leather, lie all the pieces separately on a flat surface, and cover the wrong side lightly with a layer of glue. Make sure the glue is evenly spread all over and that there are no blobs.

2 Wait for about 4 minutes until the glue is tacky, and the whiteness has gone from it. Put on the rubber gloves, take each piece of leather in your hand and scrunch it tightly into a ball, with the glue side 'inside'.

3 After about 3 minutes, ease out the pieces of leather. There will be lots of creases stuck together, but make sure that the edges are free.

4 Try the sweater on and hold some of the pieces on to your shoulder to get the right effect. The tacky glue will help them stay in position on your sweater. Ease pieces around the neck in a continuous line, and then cut the bottom edge of the leather to get a more even neckline.

5 To hold the leather design in place, use the studs. Force the legs of the studs through the leather and the wool, turn over and close. Use a *lot*.

6 To give a final dimension, use the beaded fringing. Cut into three-bead snippets, put some glue on the braided head piece and then tuck each head piece into the leather scrunches and hold down with a stud. Make sure all the different bead placements are hanging at different levels; you don't want them to look like soldiers on parade.

Tip With many of the garments in this book you must be careful when carrying shoulder bags. A heavy strap can tear, break or even remove some of your decorations (I know from bitter experience). Also be careful what you wear on *top* of many of the clothes. A heavy coat or tight jacket could squash or spoil a delicate design.

Beige Sweater with Flowers

Instead of the moulded leather flowers here, which I bought, you could make Bondaweb-backed leather flowers of your own, but they wouldn't have the same depth. The major joy – and intention – of these 'flowers on a string' is that they can be removed when the sweater is to be washed, and then re-strung. (The moulded leather wouldn't survive washing or dry cleaning.)

Time: *about 1 hour*

Cleaning: *hand wash, remove leather flowers first*

To decorate:

scraps of imitation leather (suede, lizard skin etc) and denim

gold plastic-look fabric paint

gold crochet yarn

about 5 moulded leather flowers of varying sizes

about 5 wooden beads

5 acorn or other studs

Tools and equipment:

Bondaweb

scissors

pins

iron

needle

METHOD

1 To make the leaves, I cut the various pieces of imitation leather and denim first into ovals and rectangles which I backed with Bondaweb (see page 119). Then I cut them into oak leaves of varying sizes (to complement the acorn studs I had found).

2 Try the sweater on, peel off the backing paper from the leaves, and pin them where you want them – here I have eleven leaves, sweeping down in as natural a way as possible from the largest one at the top.

3 Put the sweater on the ironing board, place greaseproof paper between sweater layers and on top of the leaves, and iron into place.

4 Keeping the paper between the layers of the sweater, outline the edges and centre of the leaves with thin lines of the gold fabric paint. This gives the leaves that embroidered look, but in half the work time – although, of course, you'll now have to leave it all to dry.

5 When dry, take the gold crochet yarn and, using it double, sew through the sweater – to the reverse and out again – at the points where you want your leather flowers to go. Use about 18 cm (6 inches) of yarn so you have a 4-strand 'tassel' approximately 9 cm (3 inches) long hanging free at the front.

6 To position your flowers, thread the four strands through the centre hole of the flower and secure by threading through a wooden bead – which forms the flower centre – and knot.

7 As a final touch – which in fact was the original inspiration for the sweater – I've added the little acorn studs, pressing the prongs through the knit at various points around the main part of the design, and closing them at the back.

Wild Things

This is the look that just happens! Basically, it's all down to your own inspiration and imagination. There is no pattern to follow, and the leather is cut haphazardly. This savage look is perfect for those who want to stand out from the crowd!

Bomber Jacket

This idea can work on almost anything. I bought the silk jacket years ago, and because there was a stain on one shoulder, I started to put some leather and fake fur decoration on – and on, and on!

Time: *for ever, if you wanted*

Cleaning: *dry clean*

To decorate:

sequin braid

lots of bits of different coloured and textured leathers and skins

about 5 sequin and bead motifs

ribbon

2 fake raccoon tails (or similar)

2 large gold buttons or beads

some shells or old earrings

piece of lace

gold beading

diamantés

Tools and equipment:

sewing machine

transparent and polyester all-purpose threads

diamanté clamping tool

METHOD

1 First of all, gather all your bits and pieces together, choosing a colour scheme to match the colour of the jacket – here they're all nice natural colours: beige, brown, coral amber, etc. Try the jacket on and play around with the potential positions, in a completely abstract pattern.

2 Working down the arm as far as my machine was capable of going, I sewed squiggles of gold sequin braid down one arm only (see page 112).

3 I chose to put my largest pieces of leather on the shoulders. I took a remnant of suede with a hole in it for the stained shoulder, and enlarged the hole to make a feature of it. I edged it with sequin braid, and sewed it in place at the top only, so that it hung loose. Also on the suede, I sewed a lovely coral-coloured beaded motif.

4 There's a green sequin leaf motif *under* the hole, and I've twisted up some orange ribbon to look (vaguely) like a rosebud. These were sewn on too.

5 To finish off that arm, I attached a fake raccoon tail. I cut off a bit of fur at the top to get a surface to sew onto; there's a big gold bead there too as an extra feature.

6 On the other shoulder and sleeve, there's a large jagged piece of imitation fur fabric, which I've sew on, but there are also lots of other bits of skin – black snakeskin, a bit of khaki python, beige suede with fringing holding a couple of suspended shells from a broken necklace. There's even a crescent of lace.

7 I've repeated the coral bead motif on the left front, but at a different angle, and the sequin leaf motif and orange rose bud on the left back shoulder. Between the latter and another shoulder-top motif, I've hung a length of gold beading. And there's another raccoon tail and gold bead on the front flap of the jacket.

Tip There's no way you could actually go shopping for the ingredients for this jacket – it's all dependent on your hoard of goodies. If you can't get hold of leather or suede, you could use artificial (or indeed any fabric), but you'll have to interlock stitch it (as I did with the fake leopard), or it will fray.

Decorated 'See-through' T-shirt

This T-shirt, a perfectly standard one, has been decorated using several techniques to give a sort of savage, jungly look. I particularly like the 'see-through' effect of the net (lace would look good too). One of the problems with plain T-shirts is that the sleeves look too full, so I've cut them with jagged edges and cut little holes using the petal technique (see page 123). This completes the look, and the fabric won't fray.

Time: *50 minutes*

Cleaning: *hand wash or dry clean* *do not iron trimmings*

To decorate:

net the same colour as the T-shirt

sequin braid to match (at least 2 m/about 2 yards)

lengths of fine braid (2 types here) to match

chamois leather pieces

scraps of sprayed leather (see page 121)

4 large beads

studs

Tools and equipment:

pins

sewing machine

transparent and polyester all-purpose threads

pinking shears

scissors

glue gun with tape or pins

studding clamp

METHOD

1 Turn the T-shirt inside out, and try it on. Wear your normal bra so that you can judge where to site the 'transparent' portions at the front – you don't want to reveal any bra cup or strap, or too much cleavage. Pin the net where you want it. I have put it in two places, one large and one small.

2 Take the T-shirt off and machine stitch the net in place round the edges in the shape you want, using a close zigzag (3 mm). You can see that the shapes are entirely random.

3 Now cut away the T-shirt fabric in front of the net shape, about 5 cm (2 inches) from the stitching on both pieces. Be very careful not to cut the net.

4 Lettuce-leaf the loose edges around both holes with the sequin braid (see page 113).

5 Cover the visible stitching all around the holes with braid (sewn on with a straight stitch). This is practical and also adds an extra dimension, particularly as I used a satin braid on the large hole, and a plaited one around the small hole.

6 Try the T-shirt on again and, using the glue gun or pins, position your leather pieces and scraps on the front around the holes at random, until you get the effect and pattern you want. It's a sort of mosaic really. Cut them to fit or to shape with the pinking shears. Before putting finally in place, cut little leaf shapes as a further decoration (see page 123). These holes reveal the colour of the T-shirt or leather underneath: I've also glued a piece of chamois *beneath* the long piece of sprayed leather so that the yellow shows through.

7 To make the fringing effects, cut regularly up strips of leather, not all the way through, and glue the head (the bit left whole) behind the main piece of leather. Add some knots to make the fringes more interesting, or some beads – here four yellow ones which clink together nicely as you move.

8 The chamois shoulder piece was cut straight on one edge and sewn along the shoulder seam (right side to right side and then folded over so that it could hang loose towards the front). Sew everything else on completely with a straight stitch, leather to T-shirt and to net.

9 The final step is to stud everything on, some at random, and some as flower or leaf patterns using the cut-out petal shapes.

Leather Fringing

You can buy this leatherette fringing in department stores, but you could, of course, do it yourself using leather or fake leather. (I always go for the easy option!) To recreate the look on a T-shirt, you need to look for one with a large ribbing band at the neck, around which you can attach the fringing.

Time: *Jeans 15 minutes; T-shirt 35 minutes*

Cleaning: *dry clean* (F) *do not iron trimmings*

To decorate:

leatherette fringing

about 100 multi-coloured beads

eyelets

glazed cotton shoelace (leather look), or any complementary cord

Tools and equipment:

measuring tape

sewing machine

transparent and polyester all-purpose threads

eyelet punch

METHOD

1 To measure how much fringing you need for the jeans, see how far down the leg you can get the sewing machine to go. You won't be able to fringe down the whole leg, particularly if they are tight jeans.

2 Sew the fringing on to the side seam of both legs (you'll need your very strongest machine needle), turning each end over a centimetre or two to neaten.

3 For the matching T-shirt, sew on the fringing, starting at the centre back, just under the ribbing seam line. Overlap a couple of centimetres when you get back to where you started.

4 Thread beads on to some of the fringes, at random. Depending on the sizes of the holes, the leatherette itself may hold them in place, or tie knots to secure.

5 To get the drawstring effect round the top, starting at the centre front, insert eyelets at regular intervals (see page 117). Thread the braid or cord through the eyelets, starting at centre front. Every time it emerges, thread on beads to fill up the gap between eyelets. Put a few beads at each end of the cord as well, and knot securely in place.

In Full Bloom

Many flower arrangers look down their noses at artificial flowers. For you, however, they will open up a whole new aspect of fashion magic. With so many varieties, colours, sizes and finishes (matt and satin, for instance), you can run riot and decorate a multitude of garments and accessories.

Firstly, though, you must buy polyester flowers, not silk. Silk flowers don't wash well: they go floppy, lose their colour, and fray. Polyester flowers, on the other hand, are *very* realistic looking. Because they're heat-embossed into curving, natural shapes and heat-cut to seal them, they never fray or lose their shape and colour when washed. They are available from florists, floral accessories shops, display shops and department stores.

Make sure the flowers have got plastic, not bound, stems, and that the backs of the flowers have little plastic 'holders' on them – which we pull off. Take hold of the petals in one hand, the calyx plastic bit in the other, and pull gently apart. The flowers will separate into layers, each with a handy hole in the middle, more expensive flowers will have quite a few layers of petals, depending on variety. Keep the leaves too.

When using flowers on your clothes, try to *think* flowers, and arrange them to look natural, as in a spray or on a branch. Similarly, remember that most flowers have yellow centres, so use yellow stones. Once you know how to attach them (see page 125) it's all so easy!

Blooming T-shirts

There are any number of effects you can achieve with polyester flowers – some simple and dramatic, others involving a combination of techniques. They are all very straightforward to make, and will give a fresh springtime look to plain T-shirts.

Beach Blossom Outfit

Brighten up a beach outfit with flowers in assorted colours and sizes, and leaves as well. You'll need small claw and large sew-on diamantés, pearl rope and studs to complete the effect.

METHOD

Use a glue gun or pins to hold assorted flowers in position on both top and shorts. Attach the small flowers with yellow claw diamantés, the larger with the sew-on ones.

On the T-shirt, I've strung some pearl rope between two little flower and leaf groups. This was sewn on behind the leaves. (Try the top on again to ensure it will fall nicely.) Scatter both top and shorts with random diamantés.

On the shorts, I've added diamantés and studs to some of the flower petals as well, the latter to keep the larger petals from drooping.

White Flower T-shirt

I printed the basic flower design on to this T-shirt – it's a puff transfer, see page 122 – but of course you could buy a T-shirt with a floral pattern already on it. The idea is to show how you can combine your blossoming flower techniques with other techniques. Choose your polyester flowers to match the colours and shapes of the flowers in the print.

Time: *25 minutes*

Cleaning: *hand wash inside out; dry flat into shape; do not iron*

To decorate:

1 floral puff transfer (optional)

a few polyester flowers in complementary colours and assorted sizes

assorted small diamantés (claw type)

a couple of larger diamantés (claw or sew-on)

studs

Tools and equipment:

greaseproof paper and iron if necessary

pins

diamanté and stud clamping tools

METHOD

1 If you're going to print the T-shirt yourself, try it on, decide where to place the transfer, and pin paper in place. Take T-shirt off and iron transfer on, following the instructions on page 122.

2 Arrange and pin the flowers where you'd like them, and clamp the smaller ones in place with yellow diamantés. Use the larger diamantés to attach the larger flowers. Scatter assorted diamantés around the design.

3 Pick out details on the printed design with studs. I've made stud veins for the leaves and some of the petals.

4 To prevent the larger polyester petals drooping, I've studded them in place at the ends. But *don't* stud them flat. Arch them before studding so that you get a more natural, curving, dimension to the petal.

Black and Red T-shirt

I think of this as a Spanish look, because of the bold contrast of black and red. A T-shirt with wide ribbing neckline and cuffs is best for this type of decoration.

Time: *15 minutes*

Cleaning: *hand wash, do not iron trimmings*

To decorate:

small red polyester carnations

yellow and red diamantés (claw type)

Tools and equipment:

glue gun with tape (optional)

measuring tape

pins

diamanté clamping tool

METHOD

1 I used the double-layer carnations here. They are quite easy to find as they're used as buttonholes. Gather them all together, and glue the bases with the glue gun. Try the T-shirt on and arrange the flowers on it to see where they look best. If you don't have a glue gun, simply pin in position.

2 Take the T-shirt off, and space the flowers out more evenly around the neck and cuffs, measuring to ensure accuracy.

3 Attach the flowers to the T-shirt through the centre, using the yellow diamantés.

4 In between the flowers, attach the red diamantés. And that's that!

See overleaf for illustrations to these instructions.

EXTRAS Attach a carnation to a clip to decorate your shoes, to match, or add to a hair slide. It's easy. (See pages 108 and 111.)

Child's T-shirt and Jeans

Look at the shapes of twigs and branches before you attempt this, and draw a design on to the garment with tailor's chalk first. You'll need plastic-look green and gold glitter fabric paints, lots of small flowers (they are called Seventh Heaven), a few larger flowers, some green leaves, some metal leaves and assorted diamantés.

METHOD

Go over the chalked twig pattern with green glitter paint on both garments. Stick on some small metal leaves with blobs of gold glitter paint. Leave to dry for at least a couple of hours.

Stick flowers and leaves on where appropriate, using the glue gun or pins, then attach with diamantés. Continue with all the flowers, mixing small and larger, until both T-shirt and jeans are complete.

54

Sweet Sophistication

Bring a touch of summer light and magic with these floral motifs which will transform your dull winter woolies. The flower theme is sure to take the gloom out of those long winter months!

Tiger Lily Sweater

A lovely way to decorate a simple sweater and make it more special. Make a matching hair-slide as well (see page 111). You'll need a spray of two tiger lilies and bud (which is how they are sold usually), two large yellow sew-on diamantés, at least a metre (a good yard) of pearl rope, and some crystal claw diamantés.

METHOD

Using the glue gun or pins, position the lilies in the centre of the shoulders, dabbing some glue on the ends of the separate petals as well. Sew the yellow diamantés to the centre of the flowers then, before breaking off the thread, sew about 40 cm (16 inches) pearl rope under the petals on each shoulder. Leave the ends dangling at different levels. Secure the tips of the petals with crystal diamantés.

Divide and cut the bud into separate petals, and dab raw ends with glue. Wrap one around each loose end of pearl rope, then sew securely in place.

As a final touch, machine-sew pearl rope along the front part of the neckline only (see page 113).

Fabric Flowers

Stun them at the gym with this fabulous tracksuit! Even if you can't touch your toes, you'll still look a million dollars in this outfit which has real 'Beverly Hills' style.

Flowered Sweatshirt

This, believe it or not, was a plain, classic tracksuit with a long-sleeved sweatshirt top, but I let myself loose on it as you can see! Now it could quite easily be worn as an evening top. With a pair of leather trousers, it would look fantastic.

Time: *about 90 minutes, not including drying time*

Cleaning: *dry clean* Ⓕ

To decorate:

gold fabric paint

gold lurex crocheting thread

gold (metallic-coloured) leather (see page 121)

Tools and equipment:

sharp scissors and pinking shears

sewing machine with leather foot

transparent and all-purpose polyester threads

pins and needles

glue gun with repositioning glue (optional)

METHOD

1 The first thing to do is to cut the sleeves off into a cap-sleeve shape. This is achieved by cutting straight across the sleeve from about 2.5 cm (1 inch) from the underarm seam to about 10 cm (4 inches) from the shoulder seam.

2 After deciding where the decorations should go, I put paper between the layers of the sweatshirt, and in gold fabric paint drew a fine tracery of branches and twigs from which the flowers and leaves would 'sprout'. They should be about the same thickness as the thread. Leave to dry in a warm place for at least a couple of hours.

3 Cut the discarded sleeves up into strips of about 5 cm (2 inches) wide and of varying lengths, ranging from about 10 cm (4 inches) to 23–25 cm (9–10 inches). These are to form the flowers.

4 Along all the sides of each of the flower 'strips', machine-sew on the lurex thread (see page 125).

5 Do the same with the rib cuffs, cutting them into strips, and edging with the lurex thread. Stretch them out when sewing, to get the lettuce-leaf effect (see page 113). The ribbing adds a different texture and the lettuce-leaf edging makes squiggly rather than smooth flowers.

6 Fold each strip in half, and wind up to form a rose shape. Don't do it evenly, the more irregular the rose the better. Sew each rose together at the base with a couple of hand stitches, and put to one side. I made 13 for this outfit. (See page 125.)

7 Cut leaf shapes of varying sizes out of the leather, using pinking shears. For this sweatshirt I made about 18.

8 Try the sweatshirt on when the paint is dry, and position the leaves where you want them, using the glue gun or pins. Machine stitch them on, curving along the centre of the leaf, using transparent thread, a straight stitch, and the leather foot. Sew two leaves on to each pocket, but leave 'flapping'.

9 Try the shirt on again, and position the flowers, pinning them in place. Sew these on by hand. Sew one on to each pocket.

10 Overlock by hand the edges on pockets and collar, using the lurex thread. Roll the sleeves back neatly to the shoulder seam line, revealing the fleecy side, and then pin into position. Overlock carefully into place with lurex thread, keeping the stitches even.

Birds of a Feather

Feathers have been used for decoration since very early times, principally by American Indians and New Guinea natives. Some magnificent feathered birds came near extinction because of the popularity of hat feathers in Europe at the turn of the century. I wonder if those ladies of high fashion ever realized that 'a feather in the cap' was an allusion to the habit of warriors adding a headdress feather for every enemy slain!

The feathers available now, however, are generally the by-product of birds raised for food – chicken, duck, turkey, etc. In Great Britain you can only acquire peacock tail feathers, not breast feathers, although these are available in France. Ostriches are reared on farms, and their tail feathers are available in rolls in haberdashery departments, but they are quite expensive.

Domestic bird feathers are dyed commercially, and if you can't find a supplier, buy feather dusters in bright colours (they're always cheap), and take apart carefully. You can make these feathers look much more exotic in a variety of ways – by spray-painting, by dyeing and by glitter-painting.

Feathers look lovely on clothes, but they are *very* delicate and don't really wear all that well. If you have to wash them, do so very carefully, dry flat and don't rub. If they need a bit of plumping out, steam them (a tip from a feather merchant). One of the best solutions is to put your feather decoration on to Velcro pads which can then be attached to the garment and taken off before the garment is washed.

Feathered Friends

I bet you never imagined that a simple feather duster could be put to such exotic use! These two items are really quick to make, so, when you've had enough of the housework, pull the duster apart and use it to work fashion magic on your clothes!

Black Feather T-shirt

I printed the cockatoo and tree trunk on to this T-shirt, but transfers as big as these are difficult to do without a proper press. You can find lots of T-shirts printed with nice birds in the shops, and this is an ideal opportunity to use feathers. You'll need clear plastic-look glitter fabric paint, which also acts as glue, 10–15 feathers in various colours and sizes, some polyester flowers and assorted diamantés.

METHOD

Put some clear glitter paint over the wings of the bird and stick on your selected feathers. Go over the loose edges afterwards with a little more paint just to seal, and then lightly brush down the feather shafts and sides. Stick four 'stemmed' feathers (see page 119) on the printed crest of the cockatoo and glitter them lightly.

I also stuck a turquoise feather to the left of the tree trunk – just for fun really!

Stick or pin the flowers (see page 125) on the branches and claw or sew a diamanté in the centre. Scatter other diamantés randomly over the designs.

Feather-fringed Skirt

This idea is simplicity itself. The suede skirt was bought with the fringes, and I've used beads and feathers to make it more fun. The necklace finishes the outfit off – see page 110 for details of how to make it. You can always buy ready-made fringing – or you can make it yourself – and sew it on.

METHOD

On the top level of fringing, slot beads on at random. You don't really need to knot, as the leather grips the beads. On each fringe you want to attach feathers to, first slide *two* beads up, then glue about 1 cm (½ inch) up on each side of the end of the fringe and stick the feather shaft on to that. Slide the beads down to cover the glued shafts, and the glue will hold it all together.

Stud the seam line of the fringe at regular intervals to accentuate it a little more.

Birds of Paradise

The following two sweaters are very dramatic and are just the thing for a night on the town. Whether you're at a smart party, or the local discothèque, you can't fail to be noticed! Walk in as proud as a peacock and watch the heads turn in your direction!

Removeable Feather Pads

These shoulder features are attached with Velcro and so are easy to remove. They're simple to make, require little sewing, and transform a plain sweater into something highly original. Use different natural colours and types of feathers for interest.

Time: *30 minutes each*

Cleaning: *Remove pads and follow garment instructions*

To decorate:

10 large feathers

about 24 medium feathers

about 40 small feathers

about 100 studs

gold plastic look fabric paint

Tools and equipment:

heavy interfacing

Copydex glue

scissors

studding clamp

10 cm (4 inch) stick 'n sew Velcro

needle and thread

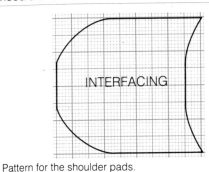

INTERFACING

Pattern for the shoulder pads.

METHOD

1 Take the interfacing, and cut 2 pattern pieces as in the pattern illustrated.

2 Glue across the curved ends of the interfacing about 5 cm in, and place 5 large feathers on each piece. The feathers will flap off the end. Work the 2 pads at the same time, so they match as much as possible.

3 Cover the base of the large feathers and the centre section with glue. Using the medium feathers, and starting in the centre with the largest, cover the bases of the large feathers closely in a semi-circular design. Let the feathers overlap slightly.

4 Cover the base of the medium feathers and the remainder of the interfacing with glue. Using the smaller feathers, start again in the centre and form a fan design, to cover the base of the feathers. Trim any loose stems that may overlap the pads.

5 Take the four pieces of velcro, and place 2 sticky pieces along either side of each pad on the reverse side.

6 Try the sweater on and position the feather pads where they suit you best. Place the other pieces of velcro in the corresponding position on the sweater, and stitch in place.

7 Squirt some gold, plastic look glue on the curved edges of the feather pads and spread it across the feathers using the stardusting technique (see page 121). Put little blobs of paint along the 'stems' of the large feathers and one on each of the medium sized feathers. This gives the look of gold beads. Leave to dry for 4 hours.

8 In the meantime, place studs around neck and cuffs of sweater as illustrated.

Pink Feather Sweater

This terrific party top is simplicity itself, and a good way of decorating a plain sweater with a rolled, off-the-shoulder collar.

METHOD

I found this wonderful sequin braid with the ostrich and cock feathers already on it – plus the bows. I just zigzag overstitched it in place.

Ostrich feathers are widely available in a roll, so you could use that to recreate the idea. Stick on contrasting feathers at intervals along the braid head, then sew some sequin braid on top to cover the new additions. Sew on some bows too if you like.

Tip To fluff up crumpled feathers hold them over the steam of a kettle and they come up like new.

64

Button and Bows

Buttons are thought of primarily as fastenings, but they can be extremely decorative too. The first necessity, therefore, is a magpie-like collecting instinct, and a good button box. Snap up cards of interesting buttons in shops and markets, snip buttons off garments before you throw them out, and look at second-hand clothes in charity shops and jumble sales – often the buttons alone justify the purchase price. None of the buttons I have used in the book were specially bought – they all came from my button box.

There are amazing button shops and departments in stores, which offer a wonderful selection of wares. Buttons come in all colours, sizes and materials – mother of pearl, plastic, wood, metal and glass – and I've even used button puff transfers in combination with some of the real thing. Buttons can decorate anything – necklines, seams, sunglasses, hair combs or shoe clips – and even the simple expedient of *changing* the buttons on a garment can transform it into something much more interesting.

Bows can be bought, already made-up and cheaply, in a variety of styles and colours, but they are simple to make at home. I have the same collecting instinct about ribbons as I have for buttons, and I have some very nice old lace ones. There's a huge selection of ribbons available, and bows made from them can tie your hair and be pinned, sewn or glued on to clothes and accessories. They are useful in a matchmaking as well as decorative capacity, too (see the section on Matchmaking).

Toss a Coin

In some Middle Eastern countries in days gone by, women would display their wealth by decorating their clothes with coins. You'll be glad to know that you don't need much money to achieve this look, just a little time and ingenuity!

Coin-decorated Top and Headscarf

Coin buttons look amazingly effective, and we've got an up-to-the-minute look here with matching top and headscarf. Don't buy buttons for the latter, as they would be too heavy. Use what are called Arabian coins – they are easily obtainable and in fact are what Arab women themselves use. You can decorate your jeans with coin buttons and chains too and get a great effect. Attach them along the waistband or around the pockets.

Time: *40 minutes*

Cleaning: *dry clean* Ⓟ

To decorate:

about 25 coin buttons of different sizes and metal finishes

thin gold metal chain

about 7 gold tassels

about 10 Arabian coins

Tools and equipment:

needles and polyester all-purpose threads

pliers

METHOD

1 On the T-shirt sew the coin buttons on in an irregular pattern round the neck, experimenting to find the number that looks right. Stitch them in place.

2 Cut the chain with pliers and attach one end to one of the end buttons (either by the link or sew it on), and then loop it three times, to the middle and end button.

3 Attach the tassels asymmetrically, two on the right side and one on the left. I bought these gold ones, but you can make them yourself. Tie the loop at the top on to a button.

4 If you don't have a suitable headscarf to spare, buy a square of chiffon to match the T-shirt and fold it diagonally to make a doubled triangle. Tie it round your head to get an idea of the length of the part you want coins on – roughly from ear top to ear top.

5 Sew the little Arabian coins evenly along this measured length so that they will hang down over your forehead. Save a few to sew on randomly on the rest of the headscarf.

Children's Clothes

All these clothes – the tracksuit top and bottom that five-year old Annabelle is wearing, and baby Alexandra's sweatshirt and trousers – came from a multiple chainstore. They're nicely made and cheap to buy, but why not pretty them up for two pretty little girls?

Annabelle's Tracksuit

Use another aspect of your artistic talents here, and carve a potato to make potato prints. I did a balloon shape – an oval with a little bit at the bottom for the balloon 'neck' – but you could try kite shapes, ballet shoes, or anything that naturally has ties and streamers.

Make a matching eyeshade by sewing a few bows and buttons on to the headband and adding the odd pearl or diamanté.

Time: *about 30 minutes*

Cleaning: *hand wash, do not iron decorations*

To decorate:

fabric paints in different pastel colours

narrow satin ribbon in different pastel colours

assorted pearls (sew-on type)

crystal diamantés (claw type)

Tools and equipment:

1 potato

paintbrush

greaseproof paper

iron

clamping tool

Make a balloon and ribbon design from a potato, using fabric paint and ribbons.

METHOD

1 Cut out your pattern on the potato, making it stand *out*, rather than *in*, and either dip into saucers of fabric paint, or brush paint on to it (to get really good edges to the design).

2 Place greaseproof paper between the layers of fabric to stop ink seeping through. Stamp your design on to tracksuit top and bottom in a few selected places – never too close together. Put greaseproof paper on top, and iron over to seal the paint (about 20 seconds). Leave to dry thoroughly.

3 Make up as many little bows of ribbons as you have balloons, and sew together, attaching a streamer tail of a different colour. Sew on to your balloons at the neck part.

4 Scatter pearls around at random – some along a yoke line if you like – and sew on. Put two little crystal diamantés on the top of each balloon, where the curve would catch the light.

Pocket detail.

Alexandra's Outfit

It's virtually all buttons and bows on Alexandra's sweatshirt and jeans, and you can see how the simplest ideas can have amazing impact.

Time: *about 20 minutes*

Cleaning: *hand wash, do not iron decorations*

To decorate:

narrow satin ribbon in various pastel colours (here lemon, pink and blue)

selected children's buttons in pastel colours

little pearls (sew-on type)

Tools and equipment:

needles and polyester all-purpose threads

sewing machine (optional)

METHOD

1 To estimate the ribbon required for the trousers, measure the pocket tops and buy 2½ times the length. (Do buy more though, as you may want matching hair bows as well.)

2 Gather the pocket ribbon up evenly by sewing along in big tacking stitches, and knot at one end. Pull and ease the ribbon to fit the pocket, then machine or hand sew in place, using a zigzag stitch as the ribbon is so narrow.

3 Make up about six to eight neat little bows from different colours of the ribbon, and sew these in various places on the trousers and top.

4 Sew the children's buttons on here and there – I found lovely little ice-cream cones, hearts, pencil stubs and sharpeners, and roller skates, which are very decorative.

5 As a final touch, scatter on some little pearls and sew them on. Never have them too close together. Put them evenly around the neck as well if you like.

Fluorescent Kid's Outfit

To create a unified look for two separate garments, button-decorate a T-shirt and jeans. It's all very easy, but the colours are important. Get *them* right, and the whole thing will fall into place.

METHOD

The large button shapes are glitter puff transfers. Cut up the transfer paper and iron them on at random over both jeans and T-shirt (see page 122). Then take as many fluorescent buttons as you like and sew them on equally randomly, but over and around, occasionally overlapping the transfer shapes. Pay particular attention to the neckline, pockets and knees – but don't put too much on the back as sitting will be a little uncomfortable.

Ribbons and Bows

This very feminine sweater has a soft, romantic look to it. Perfect for a day in the country, or wear it to the office and bring a breath of fresh air to the town. And look what a few bows can do to dress up a plain-coloured dress!

Beribboned Cardigan

This is really easy. The cardigan wasn't expensive, nor was the ribbon, and the effect is great.

METHOD

Choose a sweater with a pattern in the knit. Here there are horizontal zigzags of 'holes' across both front panels. Buy some satin ribbon of the right width to fit through the holes, allowing at least 4 metres (about 4¼ yards) of each of three complementary colours. (In fact, as I always say, it is a good idea to buy extra just to be sure: you can always make an accessory of some sort to match, for example bows on a hair slide.)

Simply thread an appropriate length of ribbon through each zigzag, alternating the colours from top to bottom, and matching each side. I knotted the ribbon at each end on the wrong side, but you could secure with some careful cardigan-colour-matched stitches. At the points of the zigzags sew on appropriately coloured bows. I made these bows myself; they're very easy, and much cheaper than buying them ready-made. If you cut the ribbons into similar lengths, the bow sizes won't vary. Sew two to two points on one zigzag, one to one point on the next and so on, to create an interesting pattern.

Evening Interest

To decorate a plain dress for evening, why not think about something like this. Well, you don't actually have to think, it's so easy! Just put safety pins on a few bows of a contrasting colour – buy them or make them up – and pin in a row down the back of the dress.

Tip This, like the embroidered sweater on page 103 is a really good way of matchmaking. The sweater here could go with a peach, brown or beige bottom half (trousers or skirt), and you could of course matchmake with a complete contrast in colours. Ribbons come in such a rainbow of colours nowadays that you can always match a colour, however unusual.

Zippy Style

I expect you thought that zips were purely functional. Well, they're not! They can be extraordinarily decorative as well, whether used simply as a zip, as a trimming, or made up into roses (see page 124). These roses are spectacular, I think, and they can also be made into earrings, hair-slides, used as shoe clips or stuck on to a bag to match a zippy outfit.

Only use metal-toothed zips. They come in all fabric colours, and the teeth are generally silver or gold finish. They come in all lengths too, but very long zips may be difficult to find. In that case you'll have to put two together or try to get some zipping trimming off a roll. (This is what the zip manufacturers use, cutting it up into the required lengths.) Zip trimming comes in basic colours, but can be dyed from white, and is usually only available wholesale – why, oh why, don't store buyers make things like this available for retail sale? I give addresses of suppliers on page 127.

When you want to add zips to garments, the only rule is always to match the metal trimming colours – gold to gold, silver to silver. And always machine-sew zips on, using the zipper foot.

Zip Along

If you've only ever associated zips with boring old anoraks, then it's time to change your mind! The following ideas will show you how to use zips for a stunning new fashion look.

Cream Rose Sweater

The pattern on this sweater made the decision about where to place the zip a little easier!

Time: *35 minutes*

Cleaning: *Follow sweater instructions*

To decorate:

1 metal-toothed zip, to measured length (see below)

1 metal-toothed zip of 55 cm (22 inches) long, for the rose

1 large silver metal button

about 20 silver studs

Tools and equipment:

measuring tape

heavy scissors

pins

sewing machine

polyester all-purpose thread

studding clamp

METHOD

1 To determine the length of the zip, you need to measure the distance from the centre front of the sweater (at bra level) up 45° to the neckline. Buy a zip about 5 cm (2 inches) *longer* than this (it's much better to cut it down than have it too short).

2 Undo the zip and divide into two halves, cutting the runners off both ends. Sew the two fabric ends of the zip together in a 'V' shape. Trim and press open.

3 Lay the sweater flat and pin the zip 'V' carefully in position, right side up, using lots of pins as the wool will stretch. (Do this over something like the ironing board so that you don't catch the two layers of the sweater.) At the ends on the shoulders, fold over the fabric part of the zip at a 45° angle (you can't fold the metal teeth) and pin. Machine sew along both sides of the zip, starting at the centre front and turning at the shoulders. Finish off neatly.

4 Make a zip rose (see page 124), hand sewing in place in the bottom of the 'V', to cover the ends of the zip underneath. Sew the silver metal button in the centre as an extra feature.

5 Stud along the fabric parts of the V zip, through both zip and sweater, at equal intervals. Measure these for complete accuracy.

Black Zip Jacket

Some fashion garments already come decorated with zips. This simple unlined jacket had zips down the arms and on the pockets. If you cannot find a zippered jacket, it's easy enough to recreate the style, *as well as* zip it up even more!

Time: *60 minutes, depending on eyelets and amount of zipping required*

Cleaning: *dry clean* **(P)** *or as advised in garment*

To decorate:

1 silver metal-toothed zip, 55 cm (22 inches) long, for roses

about 30–40 silver studs

2 silver collar tips

silver zipping lengths and pocket zips to fit (if necessary)

black braid with silver eyelets, or plain braid plus eyelets

round braid for the fringing

Tools and equipment:

needles and polyester all-purpose thread

studding clamp

eyelet punch (if necessary)

measuring tape

sewing machine

heavy scissors

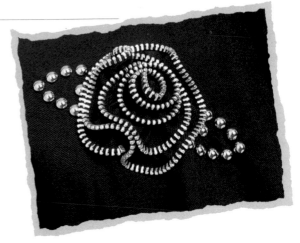

Zip rose detail.

METHOD

1 See page 124 for how to make zip roses. Sew them on in the desired places, corresponding on both sides.

2 To make the leaves for the roses, simply clamp in some studs in a leaf (triangle) shape on either side of the roses.

3 Slot on the silver collar tips (available from Western type shops), a further addition to the metal look and finish.

4 If fitting zips yourself, measure from the collar down the centre of each sleeve and cut zipping length to fit. The zip in the photograph was inserted *in* the seam, but you can simply stitch it on top, using the zipper foot. Do the same with the pocket tops, here fitting the whole zip so that it is functional.

5 Top measure for the eyelet braid (you can, of course, make your *own* eyeletted tape, see page 117), try the shirt on and work out the length of the diagonal line from about the mid-front shoulder seam to a suitable point on the placket. Double this to allow for both sides, and buy about 10 cm (4 inches) more to allow for finishing.

6 Before you sew it in place, create the fringe effect by tying two 15 cm (6 inch) lengths of the round braid into each eyelet hole.

7 Sew the eyeletted braid in place, and allow the fringe braid to hang loose and to unravel.

Eyeletted braid detail.

Zippy Denim Dress

The only 'zip' this denim dress possessed was one on a tiny pocket and two on each of the sleeves – so I've added quite considerably! I deliberately chose a dress with lots of flaps as the more it has, the more it lends itself to this sort of treatment. Remember to match the colour of your zips, studs and buttons to the colour of any existing metal trimmings.

Time: *45 minutes*

Cleaning: *Follow the manufacturer's instructions on the dress*

To decorate:

silver-toothed zips or zipping braid

3 silver buttons

silver studs

Tools and equipment:

measuring tape

pins

sewing machine

polyester all-purpose thread

scissors

studding clamp

METHOD

1 I haven't specified lengths of zipping or numbers of studs as it all depends on the type of dress you choose to decorate. Measure all edges you want to zip up and then buy zips, or zipping braid, as appropriate.

2 First of all make up three zip roses (see page 124). The top one is very tiny – made from a 20 cm (8 inch) zip – to match the scale of the small pocket, and the other two are larger, made from longer zips. The centre of each will contain a silver button.

3 Sew them in place in the desired positions, catching an appropriately sized silver button in the middle.

4 Then it's simply a case of pinning and sewing zips on to the underside of all the flaps and edges that can be decorated. Use the zipper foot, and work carefully. You will have to cut the zip if there are any sharp corners, as it doesn't turn nicely.

5 On parts where the fabric of the zip would show – on the collar here – you have to be a bit more technical. Denim collars are always doubled layered, so you should snip carefully into this layer and cut open the seam. Insert the fabric part of the zip *into* this seam, and then sew it neatly together again.

6 The final touch is to stud along all the zippered edges, as studs mix nicely with zips. Use silver studs to match the zips, and set them at about 3 cm (1¼ inches) apart.

84

Casual Zip

You can transform any casual sweater with zips. Match the zip teeth colour to any existing zip (as on the red sweater) and use any design element on the sweater as a guide to zip placement.

Feather Sweater

The basic sweater already had a zip at the neck, and the new zip goes from centre front at bra level up to the shoulders.

Time: *1 hour*

Cleaning: *dry clean* (F) *or hand wash carefully. Don't spin or tumble dry.*

To decorate:

1 metal toothed zip, to measured length

silver studs

feathers

Tools and equipment:

measuring tape

scissors

Copydex glue

pins

sewing machine

polyester all-purpose thread

studding clamp

METHOD

1 Determine the length of the new zip by measuring from centre front to edge of shoulders. Cut zip to length and sew both ends together in a 'V'.

2 Place the zip 'V' wrong side up on a table and glue from the centre about 15 cm (6 inches) up the zip on both sides.

3 Take some of the loose feathers and, one by one, stroke them downwards and place them along the glued zip so that they will hang down and the feather edges overlap slightly. The centre feather should be vertical.

4 Continue glueing and sticking feathers on the wrong side along both sections of the zip 'V'. When completed, run a light coat of glue over the top and let dry completely.

5 When dry, lay the sweater flat and pin the zip 'V' carefully in position, right side up. (Do this over something like an ironing board so that you don't catch the two layers of the sweater.) At the ends on the shoulders, fold under the fabric part of the zip to neaten and pin. Machine sew along both sides of the zip – along the top edge and also close to the zip's teeth – starting at the centre front and turning at the shoulders. Finish off neatly.

6 Take the metal studs and attach them along the zip at 5 cm (2 inch) intervals (see page 118), starting from the centre and working outwards.

Earrings

Make a pair of feather earrings to match. It's really easy. See Accessories, page 110.

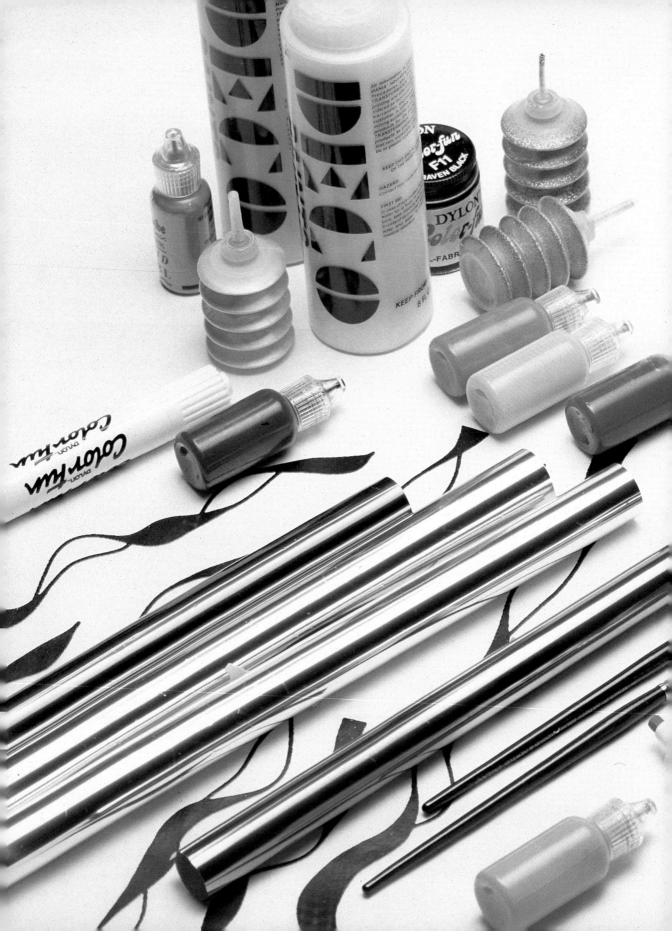

Paint the Town

There is a wonderful array of paints with which you can decorate your clothes (I talk about them in more detail on pages 120–1). You can use fabric paints or fabric paint pens, plastic-look fabric paints (which are also used as adhesives) and, rather more unexpectedly perhaps, car-spray paints! With all of these you can create some amazing effects. Do remember, though, to protect yourself, your working surface and the garment itself while you work. Paints have a nasty habit of getting where they shouldn't.

You don't need to be a budding artist to use paints on your clothes. You can buy T-shirts with printed designs already on them and 'paint' them up to make them original and individual to you. Or you can print your own at home, using iron-on transfers and foils which can then be decorated further (see page 122).

Use painting in combination with other decorative techniques to get really special effects. I've already suggested painted twigs with polyester flowers (page 54), sticking diamantés on with blobs of plastic-look fabric paint, car-spray-painted leathers, painted feathers. In this section look for the combination of foil and braids on page 90 and, the ultimate in painted clothes, the abstract top and jeans on page 91. The golden rule is to keep it as simple as you can. It's when your design gets complicated that things go wrong.

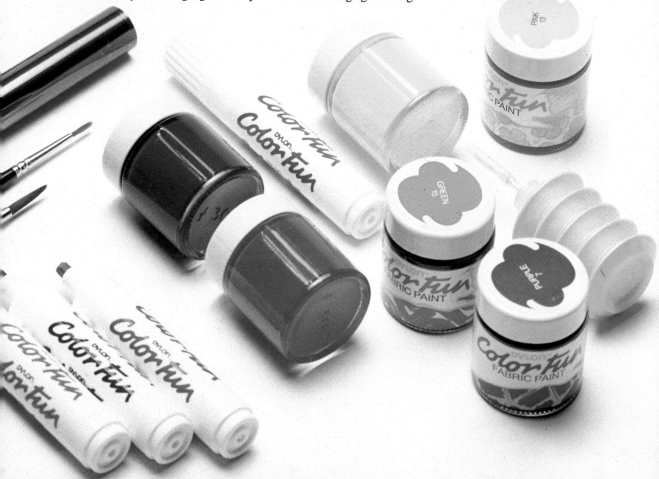

Painted Pompom T-Shirts

Two simple ideas, which illustrate how effective using paint on classic, plain T-shirts can be. Neither took me more than half an hour – although, of course, the drying took considerably longer. Buy more pompoms than you need, and use some to make a matching hair slide (see page 111).

Yellow Face T-shirt

Time: *about 15 minutes*

Cleaning: *hand wash gently inside out, do not iron directly on to paint*

To decorate:

black fabric paint pen

red puff paint, transparent glitter, blue, fluorescent orange, pink and green, and black plastic-look fabric paints

3 crystal diamantés

1 old plastic earring

painted T-shirt × 2

Tools and equipment:

tailor's chalk

iron

METHOD

1 Put greaseproof paper in between the layers of the T-shirt, and lay flat on a protected surface. Use the tailor's chalk to draw the outline of a girl's face (copy from a magazine), her eyes, nose, lips, neck etc.

2 When you're happy, go over the chalk marks with the fabric paint pen.

3 Cover with another piece of greaseproof paper and iron to set the design (see page 122).

4 Now fill in your basic design. Dust the glitter paint on the cheeks (see page 121), squeeze the red puff paint on to the lips (you'll need to iron this lightly on the reverse

when dry for it to puff, see page 120), and the blue on to the eyes.

5 Sink a diamanté into each of the eyes, and one on to a lip for extra glitter.

6 Now paint loads of hair strands using the three fluorescent colours, coming up to a ponytail point. Paint in eyelashes to match, and give her a necklace of blobs. Blob elsewhere across the T-shirt to give extra colour.

7 Stick the toning earring (clip removed) on in the appropriate place, matching the colour of the paint to the base colour – here, black. Stick pompoms on her hair using the fluorescent paints, and leave it all to dry thoroughly.

White Sunburst T-shirt

Time: *about 15 minutes*

Cleaning: *hand wash gently inside out, do not iron directly on to paints*

To decorate:

pink, orange and green fluorescent plastic-look fabric paints

6 pompoms in fluorescent yellow, green and pink

METHOD

1 Try the T-shirt on first and decide where the sunbursts are to go – they could look rather vulgar if placed wrongly! Choose two central points from which the lines will radiate, and mark in some way.

2 Lay the T-shirt flat on a protected surface and place greaseproof paper between layers of fabric.

3 With a steady hand – well, it doesn't have to be *too* steady – paint in squiggly lines of varying colours and thicknesses radiating out from the centre points. Dot a few blobs here and there if you like.

4 Stick each pompom on with paint of the same colour, and then leave the whole thing to dry.

Splash It On

What better way to get into the holiday mood than with these bright and cheerful creations?

Foil and Paint T-shirt

On a classic T-shirt, I've printed a waterfall design in metallic pink and blue, using the marbled foil technique (see page 122), and then stuck on various braids to complement the effects.

METHOD

After ironing on the transfer and foils, I cut the various braids – sequin, crocheting yarn and raffia – into lengths of about 1 m (a good yard). I put a blob of plastic-look fabric paint at the top of the design and, taking about three of the mixed strands at a time, I pressed them into the blob and let them fall across the design where they wanted to, allowing them to coil around in a natural way. The bottom ends were also sunk into the paint blobs and each blob topped with a crystal diamanté. I used all the remaining strands the same way.

Some little diamantés are scattered randomly, and some spaced around the neck.

As the sleeves were rather baggy, I cut them at an angle from the underarm to reduce the weight of material. I rolled them up and over-sewed with a fine sparkly braid.

90

Abstract Top and Jeans

This idea may look more complicated, but it's not. It's a case of using anything and everything that takes your fancy (or that you have around), and glueing it on with plastic-look fabric paint. Anything goes!

METHOD

I used different scraps of sequin braids, sequin motifs, lace shapes off an old dress, some coloured net, pieces of net with sequins (once the yoke of a dress). You could use collars, anything pretty.

Place greaseproof paper inside the clothes. Lie everything flat, and blob paint with plastic-look fabric paint on the underside of the various motifs to hold them in place.

Using plastic-look fabric paint pearlised pink, blue and lemon, I've gone round the edges of these pieces and put a blob here and there of different colours. I've then 'brushed out' the blobs with a paintbrush, mixing all the colours for a shimmering canvas effect.

I've blobbed on plastic-look glitter paint to glue on diamantés, pearl beads and other stones. The irregularity is the whole point, the whole beauty of it.

Leave to dry before cutting the sleeves as on page 90. Here I put eyelets evenly around the armholes, then I threaded silver ric-rac braid through them and looped it around the rolled-up sleeves.

Seashells

There are numerous sequins, motifs, transfers, buttons, etc to be found with a shell, seaside or marine theme, and they give a wonderful holiday feel to T-shirts, jeans, dresses – even straw bags. A very good and cheap source of natural shells is costume jewellery. I buy lovely, strung necklaces and just cut the thread, or use earrings and detach the clips with a pair of tweezers! The good thing about using 'beads' is that they have already been drilled with a hole or have a jump ring attached, so that they can easily be sewn on to a garment. If you're lucky to get real loose shells, attach them by sinking them into a large blob of plastic-look glue paint. One tip though, don't put shells anywhere where they may crush, i.e. on shoulders or back trouser pockets.

In the three styles I show here I've found marine-shaped pastel studs. They're shaped like seahorses, shells and fish and are easily attached by the two claws on the back (see stockists on page 127). On knitted and fine fabrics I put a little blob of plastic-look glue paint on the back for extra security, as fine fabrics can make them slip. They can easily be replaced by other jewellery items or button ornaments.

I recommend that all garments with shells are hand washed gently, inside-out, with a non-bleach product like Woolite. Squeeze out the excess water and dry naturally. Never spin or tumble dry!

(All instructions overleaf.)

Mermaid T-shirt

I've printed this pretty mermaid transfer on a plain white T-shirt (see Techniques, page 122). On its own, the mermaid looked just too plain and flat, so I decided to give her a beautiful marine environment and a dazzling range of jewellery! You could paint on a mermaid or a fish yourself with Dylon fabric paints and then decorate it.

Time: *45 minutes plus 4 hours drying time*

Cleaning: *hand wash, inside out*

To decorate:

1 mermaid transfer paper

gold, silver and irridescent plastic-look fabric paints

1 large yellow diamanté

yellow and blue plastic-look fabric paints

6 assorted marine studs and ornaments

80 assorted diamantés

lengths of multi-coloured pearl ropes

4 shells with jump rings (taken from earrings)

Tools and equipment:

greaseproof paper .

paintbrush

needle and all-purpose polyester thread

METHOD

1 Place a sheet of greaseproof paper inside the garment and start by giving the mermaid that sun-kissed glow! Put a little gold paint on the arms, face and body and dust it out with a paintbrush (rinse the brush immediately with cold water). Use the large yellow diamanté to create the sun, blob the stone in position with the yellow paint (see page 120) and draw the rays bursting out of it. Make the waves with the blue and silver paint, brushing the silver paint a bit to give the feeling of the waves breaking.

2 For the shells, fish and seahorses, use a mixture of the special studs and jewellery ornaments attaching them by their claws and with blobs of paint.

3 Paint on a starfish and highlight the shells and star (already printed on this design) with irridescent paint.

4 Liberally sprinkle the diamantés all over the place, and use them to put rings on her fingers and a sparkle in her eyes!

5 Leave the T-shirt in a warm, safe place to dry for 4 hours.

6 Finally, use the pearl ropes and shells to give your mermaid that dazzling jewellery collection. I threaded 3 shells on to a rope to create a dangly necklace, which I've sewn on at the shoulders. From the same points, I made further necklaces of different lengths and colours, and put the odd knot in too. I did the same thing to create the headband, bracelets and armbands. Then, I sewed on the remaining shell to create an earring.

Child's T-shirt and Skirt

This outfit is a great one to make for the children's holidays; they can even help to make it themselves!

Time: *45 minutes plus 4 hours drying time*

Cleaning: *hand wash, inside out*

To decorate:

1 transfer paper and foil

about 1 m (a good yard) green sequin rope

15 assorted marine ornaments

12 shell-shaped sequins

40 assorted diamantés

irridescent and pastel plastic-look fabric paints

Tools and equipment:

iron

greaseproof paper

METHOD

1 The transfer motifs I used here were cut from a larger sheet and ironed on, then foiled (see page 122).

2 Lay the garments flat, and place greaseproof paper inside them. Then attach the marine ornaments at random across the T-shirt and skirt, using claws and blobs of the paint to secure them. Make the seaweed by drawing the shape in irridescent paint, then sticking appropriate lengths of sequins along these lines, and putting an extra blob of paint on the ends to secure them well. Still using the irridescent paint, attach most of the diamantés and sequin shells at random across the clothes; the neckline stones should be placed at 2 cm intervals. Use matching colour diamantés for the creature's eyes.

3 With the pastel paints, work around the edges of the foil and paint scales and fins where necessary.

4 Leave to dry flat for 4 hours in a warm place and away from curious little hands!

Cross-over T-shirt

This glorious design looks good on any shape of top, and can be varied with an assortment of marine ornaments. The only rule is to keep to the three groupings and a pastel theme. Try the same idea on a sun dress too. I haven't used any paint on this T-shirt, but it goes so well with the other two that I had to include it in the photograph.

Time: *45 minutes*

Cleaning: *hand wash, inside out*

To decorate:

1 shell transfer sheet and foil (see stockists, page 127)

3 lengths of multi-coloured pearl ropes

3 shell ornaments

3 large shell sequins

3 fabric shells

60 studs

Tools and equipment:

iron

needle and polyester all-purpose thread

stud clamp

METHOD

1 The shell transfers come from a large sheet and are cut up and ironed on, then foiled (see page 122). The great thing about these particular transfers is that foil only sticks to the outline of the shells, leaving the lovely mixed pastel colours to show through.

2 As with anything involving 'hanging' ingredients, you must first try on the T-shirt to see where the pearl ropes look best. I've hung them in layers, so all are cut at slightly different lengths, then stitched in place at each end.

3 Attach a marine ornament, shell sequin and a fabric shell into each grouping. Stud inside the fabric shells, and attach them by studs. Ready-made fabric shells are available by mail order (see stockists, page 127).

4 A simple alternative to ready-made fabric shells can be achieved by backing a shiny fabric with Bondaweb, cutting into a shell shape and ironing into position (see page 119). Stud inside the shell's edge afterwards, and secure with studs to the T-shirt.

Straw Bag

To make the straw beach bag, use up some of your leftover trimmings (see Accessories, page 108).

Cooling Off

Top designers – even princesses! – are now turning their attention to glamorous swimwear, and in every department store or specialist shop you can see a colourful array of costumes and bikinis which sell for outrageous prices. However, don't be disheartened – buy cheap and plain garments, then work your own brand of fashion magic on them.

Most swimwear these days is made of Lycra, a stretchy man-made material. Because it stretches in so many different ways – depending on you and your shape – it's imperative that you try the garment on before attempting to work out any sort of decoration. Then you can stud it, diamanté it, or pin and sew on motifs. You can even cut Lycra because it doesn't fray.

All Lycra costumes will have instructions on them to rinse straightaway. Salt and chlorine are no good for the fabric, but think how much more damaging they will be to the sequins. Rinse, *very* gently, in warm water. But, that said, these costumes are not really for serious swimmers – they're more for posing around the swimming pool, sipping your *pina colada*!

Black Studded Costume with Bow Motif

This bathing costume I studded around the neckline and arms. I also used a sequin motif – a wonderful decoration for swimwear, but one which needs to be pinned on and sewn on with great care.

Try the costume on and *then* pin the motif in place. Use loads of pins because when you take the costume off, the stretched Lycra will relax again, and the motif will buckle up. Using a large needle on the machine, transparent thread in the top and self colour on the bobbin, zigzag sew around the edge of the motif *very* carefully (see page 115). Follow the pins, using them as a guide, and easing the costume in all the time. It's not easy, so I wouldn't attempt it if you're a beginner on the sewing machine.

Studded Bikini

The simplest of the lot, as I've just studded along the edges of the bikini top and bottom, as well as across some of the seams on the bottom part. The studs have gone through the elastic, but they don't affect the stretch.

Gold Flower Bikini

This too is simplicity itself. I've used the washable gold polyester flowers you find in and on Christmas decorations – a large one in the middle of the bikini top, two smaller for the sides of the bikini bottom. On all three I've pulled off the centre part – but leave the plastic stamens in, as these make the flowers stand up nicely – and sewn the flowers in place with a button through the centre. The flowers came on a stem, with leaves, so I've doubled a piece of gold pearl rope, sewn the fold underneath the flower petals at all three points, and sewn a leaf to the end of each piece of rope.

97

Orange Costume and Black and Coral Costume

These have motifs and beaded edging sewn on in exactly the same way as for the black studded costume overleaf – try the costume on, use loads of pins, then machine sew on very carefully. The decorations used are really elaborate, and not very easy to find (the sort seen on old evening dresses).

I sewed the beaded edging and its integral loop all round the top edge of the strapless orange costume. I then turned the costume inside out and carefully cut out the fabric where the hole was to be in the loop design, and stitched the edging in place from underneath.

I used exactly the same technique for the black costume, using an old coral motif with a criss-crossed hole already in it. I then cut out the fabric from the back of the hole – working carefully because of the criss-cross effect – and stitched it down in place.

Waterbaby Costume

Using claw diamantés as here, you could write any appropriate heat or water words – such as SPLASH, WET or IT'S HOT, to quote but three! Try the costume on, work out the area you want to cover with your wording, and then make a stencil to size (see page 118). The stencil is then rubbed on to the reverse of the costume, and the claws are pushed through to the front and the diamantés inserted. Because the diamantés are put on individually, they don't affect the stretch, but do work each letter in stages, six claws through at a time perhaps, before inserting diamantés and closing the claws. It's really very easy!

Matchmaking

In a sense, the whole book is about matchmaking. In most of the chapters, whether I'm talking about paints, glitter, flowers, feathers or buttons and bows, I'm using decorative techniques to create a unity, to make one garment relate to another.

Colour matching is often difficult. If you've bought something and have absolutely nothing to go with it, you can matchmake with braids, yarns or ribbons, all of which come in a rainbow of colours. That's what I did for the pink suit on page 103, adding some very basic pink embroidery to a black sweater to tie it all together. You could do the same thing with a colour-matched ribbon, threading it through an open knit or through the seam holes that you often see in sweaters.

Remnants can be used to matchmake. In two instances here, I've used cut-off hems to create a matching top. Because I'm so small, I'm constantly taking up hems, and I like using the cut-offs in this way. You might, with the vagaries of fashion, want to *lengthen* a hem, so a gypsy flounce could be the answer. I did this to the evening dress overskirt on page 104, which transformed it from a fairly dull dress into something much more glamorous. The additional fabrics used may be rather pricy but as you only have to buy one metre your evening dress will be a bargain!

Use accessories, too, to help you matchmake. This is where they are all-important.

Outer Space Sweater

Bought trousers or jeans for children are often too long, and you have to take them up. Here is a way of using the cut-offs to make an interesting and kid-approved matching outfit. It's an excellent idea for either a sweater *or* a T-shirt. In fact the kids could do it themselves, it's so easy.

METHOD

Cut the bottom of both legs to size, and hem the jeans to fit. Put some Bondaweb (see page 119) over the cut-offs and iron to adhere. Cut this into the shapes that you fancy – here a rocket, stars and crescent moons. Arrange these on the sweater and mark position with pins. Tear paper off the back of the Bondawebbed shapes, and iron down into position. The edges won't fray, but here, to further seal and decorate, I've gone round them with green plastic-look fabric paint.

102

Embroidered Sweater

Even if you shudder at the memory of those ghastly table-mats we had to sew at school, you can still match-make a difficult suit or outfit. It's easy, and the stitching doesn't have to be perfect. A plain black sweater with this pink suit would have looked too harsh on its own, so I sewed some basic little patterns on to the sweater with matt pink tapestry wool.

METHOD

There was already some embroidery on this particular common-knit chainstore sweater, so I could follow that to an extent. I've oversewn some shapes, outlined others, picked out leaf veins in pink, and made little tassels which I stitched down at the top. I've oversewn the neck evenly as well.

There are no rules at all, but do try the outfit on first to see where the colour decoration is needed. It might be appropriate on yoke, shoulder seams, hem or cuffs.

Layered Evening Dress

Another aspect of match-making is adapting and improving. This black satin strapless evening dress was very cheap and not of very good quality, but with a metre of printed chiffon and half a metre of a gunmetal silver material, I've transformed it into a stunning party number.

METHOD

I machine-sewed the chiffon into a circle and gathered it at the top. This I sewed on to the waistline of the dress, using the same technique as for attaching beaded lace (see page 21). I eased the gathers to fit, then folded over to hang over the original skirt.

I cut the gunmetal material in strips to make it twice the measured length of the overskirt hem diameter. This made the ruffle. Sew into a circle and hem top and bottom. Gather one side and sew to the bottom of the overskirt, easing gathers to fit, and leaving about 5 cm (2 inches) as a little ruffle on top.

For the bodice, I've cut little strips of the gunmetal fabric, folded them in half, and gathered them too. I've unpicked the top seam of the bodice and eased in my tiny ruffle, then oversewn.

The matching sash is hemmed on both long edges and ends, and it ties at the back. I've put some silver thread in the eyelets to add interest at the bustline.

Scalloped Matching T-shirt

This is a really quick and easy thing to do. I took a maximum of half an hour to create a new outfit from an old patterned skirt that needed shortening and a classic round-necked T-shirt of a complementary colour. Any patterned fabric could be used – fruit and butterflies, etc, and anything you can use in a similar 'scalloped' way around the neck of the T-shirt complements the garment still further.

METHOD

I cut the skirt to length, backed the offcut material with Bondaweb and cut round the pattern of the flowers to make pieces about 15 cm (6 inches) in length. Then I tried on the T-shirt and pinned on the flowers to create a new 'V'-shaped neckline. I ironed each one on individually, and then cut around the top edge of the design a fraction – 3 mm (1/8 inch) – to neaten.

Purely for decorative purposes, I went round all the edges of the flower designs with thin lines of gold plastic-look glitter paint to create an embroidery effect. This defines the edges, giving the whole thing a bit of a lift. Do the front first, giving it at least 1½ hours to touch-dry before doing the back. Then leave for about 4 hours to dry completely.

Accessorize

Accessories make the outfit, so they say, and I agree. Nothing makes an outfit look more put together than the judicious use of a matching hair slide or comb, earrings or shoes. As I've been saying throughout the book, always buy *more* than you need for a particular outfit, and you can use the leftovers for a wealth of accessories. None of the items photographed in the book is difficult or lengthy to make, and they all make an incredible difference. But, do please remember that these accessories are fun things, to match your new fun outfits, and they're not made to last. They come in for a lot of handling, so you may need to re-glue or repair for a repeat wearing. However, if you are wearing an already-decorated outfit, don't go wild with decorated accessories – they'll only detract from your work of art.

Bags

Leather is difficult to work with because of the shape of bags, and because it would not be easy to push needles through, but you could, of course, glue items on to an old leather bag, or clip on a decorated shoe or earring clip (the principle of those wedding bag decorations made up by flower arrangers). In general I use fabric or straw, on which any of the items – flowers, feathers, shells, sequins, sequin motifs, zip roses etc – could be used.

The little peacock feather bag was made of plain pleated satin, and I pinned on a circle of extra bought pleated satin braid. Then I made a cross with a couple of peacock feathers – cut down to the 'eye' on the feather – and sewed on a lovely irridescent sequin motif and some beaded fringing. It took me a maximum of half an hour, and I think it looks spectacular.

With straw bags, you can go to town – or the beach, rather, because they're ideally suited to relaxed holiday usage. Use transparent or pearlised plastic-look fabric paint to stick items on but, depending on the looseness of the weave, you may need to put greaseproof paper inside the bag so the paint doesn't seep through. On one (see page 50) I've used a whole load of leftover flowers and leaves, on another (see page 92) shells and pieces of paint-scrunched fabric, for an interesting creased effect. I put blobs of three different colours of the paint around the edges of the fabric pieces, then brushed them together (as for the T-shirt and jeans on page 91). Then I stuck on shells and little fish-shaped studs.

Belts

As for bags, leather is difficult to work with unless you use glue – and decorative items would be knocked off rather easily. Thin leather belts can be studded, of course, which would be more permanent.

The most important thing is that the belt should harmonise with the outfit – there's a huge variety in leather, fabric and cord that can be bought. You can also use other things to achieve this harmony, such as a chiffon scarf with an earring clipped on to it, as for the child's outfit on page 104, and a length of the same material as for the evening dress on page 104.

Shoes

Once again, leather is difficult to decorate unless you use shoe or earring clips, both of which are easy and cheap to buy. Build up your design on the back of the clip, glueing it solidly in place, and then clip in front or – much less conventional, and much more interesting – clip in groups around the shoes as for the red flowers on page 52.

The shoes I decorate most are those canvas sneakers or gymshoes that you can buy incredibly cheaply. And on them I've used blobs of plastic-look fabric paint to glue on sequins, bows, shells, stars, little diamantés, tiny flowers – whatever I have around. Be careful not to put anything on the front of the shoe where it will bend or crease, and don't use anything too big on the front either. It'll just fall off when you walk. I've put tiny blobs of plastic-look fabric paint in different colours along the edges of some soles too. Leave all to dry well, at least overnight, before wearing. A final touch is to replace the existing laces (if appropriate) with a contrasting colour – much more fun.

Miscellaneous

Although I haven't illustrated any hats, plain straw or felt ones could easily be decorated using many of the techniques and materials described elsewhere in the book. Scarves can be decorated too (see the coin scarf on page 69), and for a child's eyeshade, simply glue on appropriate decorations as on page 70.

A glittery bow tie and pair of gloves would give a touch of fashion magic to any fun outfit. Use claw diamantés on the bow tie (impossible to iron on with a domestic iron because of the thickness of the folds). Put greaseproof paper inside the net gloves and then iron on diamantés in your chosen pattern (here the classic stitch pattern you get on most gloves). Turn the gloves over and iron again from the other side to be sure the diamantés adhere properly. Sew on a little bow to finish each glove off, here of some silver ric-rac braid.

A tasselly idea finally. Stockings or tights with ankle motifs are all the rage – so why not make your own? Gently sew tassels that complement your outfit to the seam at the back of a pair of tights or stockings, so that they hang just to the top of your most glamorous high heels. If and when the stockings or tights ladder, just unpick the tassels and use them on the next pair!

Jewellery

I've mainly concentrated on earrings, as I think they're so easy to make, and look so good. Necklaces somehow look too fussy with the sort of clothes I transform – except with, say, *bustiers* and low-cut tops. Neither have I made any brooches for the outfits here, but they could be made in exactly the same way as the earrings I describe below, using brooch pin fittings instead of earring clips.

Basically with earrings, what you do is either buy earring clips (from people who supply jewellery findings, department stores etc), and build your design on them, or you buy cheap plain plastic earrings on to which you stick your own decorations. (On the whole, clips are more appropriate than pierced ear earrings, because of the weight of most items.)

Flower earrings are made this way: glue the flower on, using Superglue or plastic-look fabric paint, top with a diamanté, and leave to dry. If you are using plastic-look fabric paint, after 2 hours push in the diamanté to be really sure the flower is gripping the base properly.

Zip earrings can be made from smaller lengths of zip exactly as for the zip roses on page 124: sew them together at the back instead of on to a dress, then glue on to the clip or earring.

For dangly earrings, you can use tassels: simply twist the tassel top through sleeper earrings. You can also use lengths of beaded braid, glueing the end firmly to a small clip or pierced ear earring.

For feather earrings, you need to double a small length of cord or soft leather, and slot on some beads. Glue feathers to the ends of the cord and then slide the beads down over the ends of the feathers to conceal the raw ends. Suspend the loop from an appropriate earring.

There *are* a couple of necklaces here, one a simple length of beaded braid (see page 31), to which I've attached a fastening, and a feather one to match the fringed skirt on page 61. For this, I've simply taken a length of the fringing and attached feathers and beads as for the skirt, then twisted a narrow length of chamois leather in and around the top of the fringing to add an extra dimension. It ties simply at the back.

Hair Decorations

There are loads of basic hair decorations which can be bought, and then decorated even further to match your outfits. Think of combs, slides and those spring-clips, for a start. Obviously the bigger the area each clip has to be decorated the better. It's a case of glueing again – although you'll have to judge the weight and some heavier items might need to be *bound* on – and using leftovers or delving into your colour-coded boxes. Use Superglue or plastic-look fabric paint to stick on sequin motifs, sequins, diamantés, scrunched leather pieces, feathers, flowers, bows, pompoms, small zip roses – anything that's pretty and that's lying around.

A particularly nice idea for hair is to have dangly bits – some leather or fabric fringing, pearl rope or beading (with a bud attached to echo that on the lilac sweater on page 55). I first made hair spring-clips for myself in the south of France to go with jeans, and a customer who saw them immediately ordered a hundred. I was delighted, not least because I was literally using bits and pieces picked off the floor!

You can buy slides with flowers already on them, and these I take off, replacing them with flowers to match an outfit. These slides have a prong on them which the flower slots on to. Always use the plastic stamens as well on hair decorations, and never throw away the flowers you've removed – put them in your colour-coded boxes and save them for another day!

The feather decoration on page 47 was made in a slightly different way: I took a piece of beige cord, about 30 cm (12 inches) long, and threaded some beads on. I then glued feathers on to each end and slid the beads on top to hide the feather ends (very similar to the earrings in fact). Use the cord to tie your hair up, or attach to an elastic band.

The hair decoration to match the yellow tracksuit on page 57 was made with a strip of the fabric, about 25–30 cm (10–13 inches) long and 5 cm (2 inches) wide. Fold this in half inside-out and then straight-stitch along the long seam. Then turn the right way round and slot through a piece of elastic, half the length of the strip. Catch at each end, and then sew the ends of the strip and the elastic neatly together to make a stretchy circle. I then sewed on a yellow rose to match those on the tracksuit top. Adapt this idea to any leftover pieces of fabric – I use the trouser and skirt bottoms that I'm always having to cut off because I am so small, and they really finish off an outfit's look.

Techniques

There are a few applying techniques used in the book that you might need a little help with. I have also included a few hints here about some of the decorations and tools used.

Practise the techniques you need on scraps of material until you get the hang of them. They take a little time to perfect and the times I give in the instructions do assume a certain level of confidence and expertise! Obviously, the more you practise, the quicker you will become.

Certain fabrics may have to be backed with the appropriate weight of interlining before you start. Attaching decoration to chiffon, for instance, is very different to working with denim.

The techniques I describe here are all suitable for the beginner. However, if you are thinking of going into business and making up dozens of your designs, then you will want to invest in more sophisticated, time saving equipment (see page 127).

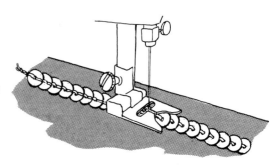

Machine sewing.

Applying Sequin Rope

Individual sequins come ready-strung on a rope, so they can be stitched on quickly. These give a professional finish that would normally take hours of fine handwork. They can be bought easily by the metre in haberdashery stores and departments.

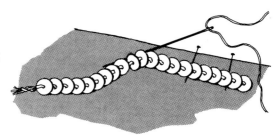

Hand sewing.

Machine Sewing

To apply them along a seam or as pure decoration, put transparent thread in the top of your machine, and polyester all-purpose thread of the same colour as the sequin rope in the bobbin. Use a size 80 needle (ball-point for jersey and T-shirts). Check the sequins are in the correct overlap position and, using a large straight stitch, machine along the centre, guiding the sequins with your right hand. Stitch very slowly. Sew in the same direction as the sequins overlap.

Hand Sewing

If stitching by hand, use matching polyester thread, pin in place, and catch the 'rope' that holds the sequins together from behind as shown.

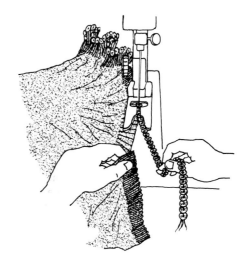

Sewing lettuce-leaf edging.

Lettuce-leaf Edging

Sequinning edges gives a very attractive and feminine touch to sweaters, T-shirts and other fine knit fabrics (see page 28). It is probably the most difficult technique in the book, and you should practise before going directly on to the garment. (Practise with thick string on old sweaters and T-shirts.) Use the same threads and needles as above, but put the zigzag on its widest stitch and adjust the length to 3 mm (⅛ inch).

1. Place the sequins in the correct direction – so you sew in the direction of the overlap – and lie over the knitted edge so that the knitted edge lines up with the rope that holds the sequins together.

2. Machine a few stitches to hold in place, with the zigzag crossing on the right from the centre of the sequin over to the left of the fabric.

3. Use your right hand to guide the sequin rope, keeping it slightly raised and, with the left hand, stretch the knit firmly forward.

4. Machine sew to the stretched bit as far as you can go before your hand hits the machine. Then take up a further bit of rib and stretch and sew. You're pulling against the natural feed of the machine – imagine you're trying to pull it *out* of the machine. The rope is sewn on to the stretched rib, and when that rib comes back to its normal tension after the needle has caught the rope, it will ruffle up. This is what creates the ruffle effect.

5. At the end, when completing an edge, overlap a few sequins, reverse a few stitches, and cut threads and sequins.

Applying Pearl and Diamanté Ropes

Moulded pearl and diamanté ropes are a cheat's dream! They appear to have been carefully strung by hand, but are actually bought by the metre, and each pearl or diamanté has been moulded on to a centre cord. This makes it easy to cut to the desired length without everything falling off (as with a string of pearls or beads).

Machine Sewing

Set the machine at the longest and widest zigzag stitch. Use a size 120 needle and have transparent thread on the top of the machine and matching polyester all-purpose thread in the bobbin. Line up the centre of the machine foot with the trimming and stitch slowly, letting the needle cross over the rope without actually touching it. These trimmings do not fray when cut, so you can cut to the exact length when you have reached the end.

Hand Sewing

Overlock with transparent thread at each point between pearls or diamantés.

Lettuce-leaf Edging

Do exactly as you would for sequin lettuce leafing (see opposite), but sew to the extreme edge of the fabric. The finished effect is more rigid than with sequin braids, and looks excellent on a peplum as it will make it stand out!

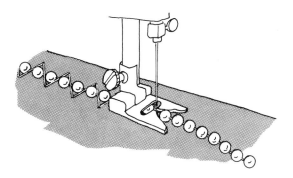

Machine sewing pearl rope.

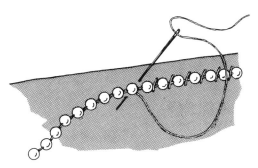

Hand sewing pearl rope.

Applying Beaded Nets

These braids come ready-beaded which means you don't have hours of tedious hand sewing, and they can be easily attached to give a very professional finish. They are also available as collars and yokes. They gather easily.

They should be stitched with either a hand or machine straight stitch with the net laid beaded (right) side to the right side of the garment, but in the opposite direction to which you want it to fall.

When you have pinned and sewed in position, trim the raw edge to about 2 cm (⅝ inch) to neaten (it doesn't fray), then turn the net over and down to its correct position. Topstitch, or cover with braid as on page 21.

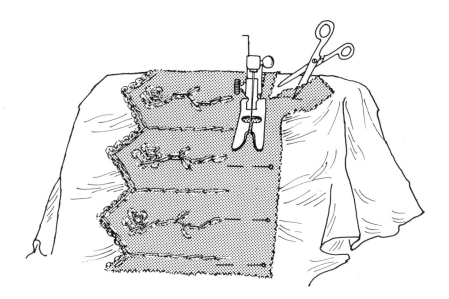

Pin and stitch right sides together.

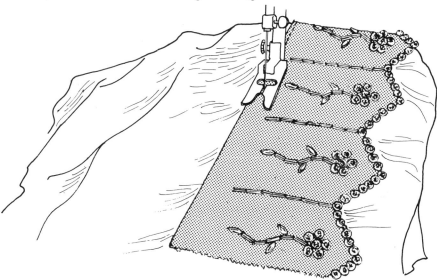

Trim excess lace, then turn and topstitch.

Attaching Sequin Motifs

Sequin motifs save a lot of tedious hand sewing, and have infinite uses. There are a variety of different designs in many metallic and matt colours. Generally they are hand beaded in the Far East and consist of an outline of bugle beads filled in with sequins. These normally overlap and it is very important for machine sewing that you sew in the same direction as the overlap. If you accidentally go against this, the sequins will catch, split and fall into the sewing machine.

When pinning sequin motifs in position, use pins with coloured tops, and count how many you put in. It's very easy when the garment is finished to miss one – and you may find it again rather painfully!

Pin the motif in position.

Machine Sewing

You need transparent thread in the top of your machine and a matching polyester all-purpose thread in the bobbin. Change the needle to size 110 or 120 so that, if the needle hits a bead, the bead will break rather than the needle, leaving the thread intact. If you use a finer needle, it will break constantly. (Before I worked all that out, I'm sure I kept needle manufacturers in business, I used so many!) Change your needles regularly as well, as this type of work blunts them easily and can cause irregular stitches. (Needles can be sharpened by running ordinary sandpaper through the machine.)
1. For all fabrics except jersey and T-shirt cottons, set the machine at the longest and widest zigzag stitch. Machine as shown in the direction of the sequin overlap, with the needle crossing from the motif to the fabric. Manoeuvre the fabric at the same time. When completed, overlap the starting point and cut threads.
2. When machine sewing jersey and T-shirts, use a size 80 ball-point needle and set the machine at the longest straight stitch. Using the same threads as before, sew *inside* the sequin motif as shown, keeping the needle clear of large beads. This is to prevent the T-shirt or jersey material from going into holes. (It is not advisable to attach all bead motifs on to these fabrics by machine sewing; hand sewing or ironing Bondaweb on the wrong side may be better.)

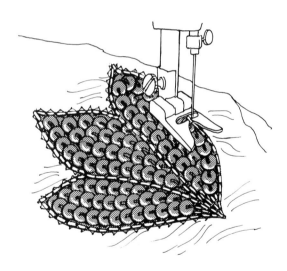

Machine with zig-zag stitch in direction of sequin overlap.

Hand Sewing

Overstitch the edge of the motif, using a transparent thread.

Glueing

Use plastic-look fabric paints for glueing small motifs only (see page 120). Always make sure that this is the last process, as the paint needs 4 hours to dry.

115

Diamantés

Diamantés add sparkle to anything. They can be scattered in a random way over a garment, or placed close together to form regular designs, letters or words. (You'll need a stencil for the latter, see page 118.) They come in a multitude of colours, varieties and sizes and are made of glass or plexiglass.

Loose Stones

These can be attached simply by sinking them into small blobs of plastic-look fabric paint, or by using matching claws which you buy with the stones.

1. To attach diamantés with claws, mark the desired position with a pin, pushing it through the fabric from the right side. Push the claws through the fabric from the wrong side over the end of the pin (each fitting has a hole in the centre).

2. Remove the pin and drop the diamanté on to the claws.

3. To fold the claws over the stone, use a diamanté clamping tool which pushes down on to the four claws simultaneously. If you can't find such a tool, use a small screwdriver.

Pre-set Stones

These are stones which are bought already set in their claws. The claws are pushed through the right side of the fabric and closed on the wrong side with a clamping tool (or screwdriver).

Iron-on Stones

These have adhesive on their flat backs. When applying you must put greaseproof paper between layers of the garment to prevent this adhesive going through where it shouldn't. There is a handy little gadget which you hold over the stone for about 10 seconds; this concentrates the heat like a wand, and you don't have to worry about the heat affecting any other part of the garment. It is available by mail order (see page 128), but many of you will have to rely on a domestic iron.

1. To apply iron-on stones, insert greaseproof paper between layers of the garment.

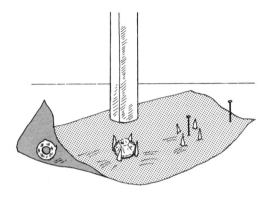

Use clamp to secure diamantés.

2. Place your garment flat on the ironing board and arrange your design of diamantés. Lay another piece of greaseproof paper on top.

3. Place the iron – heated to its hottest setting – over the design and hold there for about 20 seconds.

4. Because this first heat application will only just hold the diamantés in place, turn the garment inside-out carefully and iron on the reverse side of the fabric, again through paper, for another 20 seconds on the flat part of the stones. Dark spots should appear on the wrong side of the fabric where the glue is seeping through. You could put the garment over the free end of the ironing board.

5. If you make a mistake, simply heat the stone again as above, and move while the glue is liquid. (It may leave a mark, but it depends on the fabric.)

Sew-on Stones

These are the larger ones. They have holes in two sides and must be hand sewn on. Many diamantés are available on button mountings.

Eyelets

Eyelets are a great decoration that lend themselves to lacing, and are a good way of introducing new colours to an outfit. Make sure the colour of the eyelets matches that of other metal trimmings (ie zips and buttons, etc). Eyelets are also available in enamel colours. They can be bought from haberdashery departments along with the attaching gadgets.

To make eyelet tape, apply evenly to plain white tape.

Woven Fabrics, Braids and Leather

1. Mark the positions first.
2. You need to pierce a hole with a leather hole punch (as shown). This hole should be smaller than the eyelet (the gun has piercers of various sizes): with a loose weave the hole should be on the smallest setting, and on leather it should be fractionally smaller than the eyelet. You need to experiment on a scrap of similar weight material first – the hole should hold the eyelet without it slipping out. If it is not possible to do a practice run, start with the smallest hole, moving up until the correct tension is found.
3. Push the eyelet through the hole from the right side and place the eyelet punch over from the wrong side (as shown) and gently squeeze.

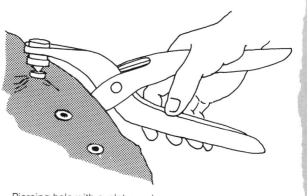

Piercing hole with eyelet punch.

Making hole in knitted fabrics.

Knitted Fabrics

For a loose knit it is not necessary to pierce a hole but gently push the eyelet through the knit. Each eyelet should be pushed in individually.

For knits like T-shirts, a small washer must be used underneath when closing – this stops the fabric laddering. Alternatively, some interlining can be ironed on underneath the desired position (ie when a strip or pattern of eyelets is to be done).
1. For jersey and T-shirts, start by marking the positions of the eyelets.
2. Take a stitch unpicker and catch a single thread in the desired position. Gently pull and cut the thread.
3. Immediately put the eyelet through the hole, stretching the fabric tautly across it. Then use the punch to close the eyelet.

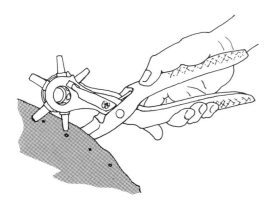

Making hole with leather punch.

Studs

A variety of studs and nailheads are available in various metal and antique finishes. Check they are made of brass as these can be washed easily and do not rust. Scatter them on any garment together with a metal trimming of some sort (metal buttons, zips, eyelets etc), and always match them to the trimmings. If you are working to a pattern, see opposite for how to make a stencil. Do all your studding on a hard or firm surface – and if it's your best wooden table, protect it first.

Two-pronged nailheads are pushed through the fabric from the right side and the claws folded across under the stud. It is best to wear a thimble to protect the forefinger!

The small four-pronged nailheads that are used in the book are the most secure, and offer the largest variety of design. These are also pushed through from the right side, and closed with a studding clamp. Simply push this down on to the claws, and all four will close simultaneously. Or use a screwdriver to fold the claws over.

If the studs are to be placed in a more awkward position – on a pocket for instance – push the stud through and hold firmly with the back of the thumb. Turn the individual claws back with the clamp or a small screwdriver.

If you have made a mistake, and want to remove the stud, carefully ease a blunt embroidery needle under each claw from the wrong side and ease open. Very gently remove the stud from the other side without pulling.

If you want to stud knitted fabric (see page 27), put iron-on interfacing under the area before studding.

Stencils

For a special formalised design, whether using studs, diamantés or blobs of paint, you need to make a small stencil.

Diamanté Stencils

1. For stud or diamanté shapes, put a piece of tracing paper over the garment or fabric in the desired position, and experiment with loose stones to form a design.
2. When you are satisfied, mark the position of each stone on the paper with a pencil.
3. Put the stones aside and punch over the marks with a pattern-making punch (available from good stationery shops).
4. Depending on the type of stud or diamanté you are using, transfer the design on to the right or wrong side of the fabric, by rubbing over the holes with tailor's chalk. This will leave blobs of chalk where the holes are, and will show you where to apply your stones accurately.

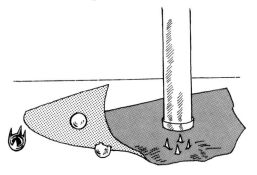

Closing stud with a studding clamp.

'Stemmed' Feathers

Hold a feather in one hand and, with the other, pull off the bottom two thirds of the feather vanes towards the quill end of the shaft – lots of firm but gentle tugs downwards, working a bit at a time, on each side. You will be left with a pretty plume at the top of the shaft.

'Stemmed' feathers.

Dyeing Feathers

They can be simply sprayed with metallic colours, using gold or silver car-spray paint (see page 121). To dye the feathers of land birds, use a simple fabric dye. The same dyes can be used for feathers from water birds, like geese, but the feathers must be cleaned of the oils first. Do this by boiling them in a strong detergent, then use the dye in the normal way.

Glues and Adhesives

Because I hate sewing, I use glue a lot. Plastic-look fabric paint, which acts as adhesive as well as paint (see page 120), was truly a revelation! The other glues I use are Copydex, Superglue and Superglue gel, and the ATG 100 Scotch glue gun. Adhesive products used in the book are interfacing and Bondaweb.

Copydex

This is by far the best glue for leather and feather work. For porous surfaces, apply to one surface only; press firmly and allow to dry. For non-porous surfaces, apply sparingly and evenly to both surfaces; allow to become touch dry (about 15–20 minutes), then bring together firmly. Do not dry clean.

Superglue and Superglue Gel

Both glue and gel are good for jewellery – earrings and shoe clips for instance. Take care not to get the glue in contact with the fingers as it bonds permanently in seconds. It's best on non-porous surfaces. The gel is the same, but with a thicker and tackier consistency which I prefer.

Glue Gun

This is a fairly new product, an implement of about 23 cm (9 inches) in length, which has a roll of special sticky tape inside it. It can be bought from stationery shops. I find it particularly useful because the glue – basically the same as that on conventional sticky tape – is non-permanent, staying tacky for ages, which means that you can *re-position* items. When trying a garment on in front of the mirror, instead of pinning things on, you can glue them and move them around endlessly until you're happy. Then you attach them in a more permanent way.

You often have to *push* the item against the gun, particularly the polyester flowers. Then pull the item off, bringing the glue off the cellophane tape.

Bondaweb and Interfacing

These are invaluable in several areas of fashion magic – the applique T-shirt on page 105, for instance, could not have been achieved without Bondaweb. This is a sheet of parchment paper holding a wafer-thin layer of glue. To use, place on the wrong side of the fabric, shiny paper side up. Iron all over for about 20 seconds, and the heat melts the glue on to the fabric. Allow to cool. Now you can cut out your shape or motif (if relevant). Peel off the layer of shiny paper, place the motif in position, and re-press. There's no sewing involved – a particular plus for me – and a further advantage is that cut-out motifs will never fray, the Bondaweb glue having fused all the threads together.

Interfacing is used for stiffening and to protect fabrics like T-shirt cotton from laddering when holed (as with eyelets, see page 117). It is like Bondaweb, but is a thin webbing with glue on one side only. Place the shiny glue side on to the fabric and iron over.

Using Dylon Fabric Paints

If you can paint your face you can paint your clothes. There are a few rules, though. Most fabrics, natural or man-made, can be painted, but not acrylic, polyester (Terylene), wool jersey, tweed, or rubber-based fabrics.

If the garment is new, it must first be washed clean of any manufacturer's finishes – then dried and ironed. Before you start, protect yourself with overalls and rubber gloves; protect your working surface (floor, ironing board, table) with blankets, polythene, newspapers or sheeting.

The garment or fabric to be painted should be laid flat on the protected surface, with greaseproof paper or polythene between layers, and pinned or taped in place.

One method we use in the book is potato printing (see page 71), which will serve as an example of the basic fabric paint technique.
1. Cut an appropriately sized potato in half and cut out your *raised* pattern with a small sharp knife. It should be about 12 mm (½ inch) deep so that the paint won't come on the *un*patterned bit.
2. Put the paint colours in separate saucers at your side (or you can, of course, *mix* colours). Wipe excess moisture off the cut end of the potato first and have a few practice runs with the chosen pattern. Do this on a spare bit of material or a place on the garment that won't be seen.
3. Starting at the top of the garment, press the potato pattern into the paint, without overloading it, and press down firmly on the fabric. Lift up immediately. (If your print needs well defined edges, like the balloons on page 71, use a brush to apply the paint.)
4. Repeat this for each piece of pattern, and allow the painted side of the garment to dry thoroughly before painting the second side.
5. To set the fabric paints, and make them washable and dry-cleanable, iron all parts of the painted fabric at the hottest setting through greaseproof paper or cotton sheeting for 2 minutes. Do this when all patterns on the garment are completely dry.

Using Plastic-look Fabric Paints

Plastic-look fabric paints that stick come in primary, fluorescent, glitter and pearlised colours, and can be used as paint and as adhesive (see page 127 for different makes). They can be used on virtually all fabrics and leather as well as on paper, cardboard, glass, wood and metal, and you could decorate shirts, trousers, hats, gloves, shoes, sneakers, socks, underwear etc. They are available from craft shops, artists' materials suppliers and large department stores.

They come in small plastic bottles or tubes, and there are several methods of applying them when using to decorate your clothes. Put greaseproof paper between layers of garment to be painted.

Blobbing

This technique is used for sticking on small items – stones, motifs and small swatches of fabric or leather. Squeeze directly from the bottle a blob 3 mm (¼ inch) thick which is larger than the area of your stone or motif. Place the item gently on the blob and, using the point of your scissors or any fine pointed instrument, sink the item in, prodding firmly.

Blobbing in miniature can also be used as a decorative finish around necklines of T-shirts, on shoes, and to write words or names.

Brushing

This gives a good artistic look, and is very easily achieved. A paintbrush and a pot of water is all that's needed. Keep rinsing the brush as you go. Pour the paint out of the tube directly on to the fabric and spread with the brush over the chosen area.

To apply larger fabric swatches (as for the T-shirt and trousers on page 91), put a little paint along the edges of the swatch on the wrong side. Turn on to the fabric and press down with your fingers. Now squeeze blobs of paint along the edges of the swatch – don't be afraid to mix them – and brush along as you go. Don't let the brush become clogged: rinse in water and dry with a rag.

Dusting

A technique for glitter paints, which creates a spray of glitter. Squirt a fine line about 5 mm (2 inches) long, directly on to the garment. Then, using a firm piece of card, wipe the straight edge through the paint and across the garment. This dries very quickly as there is no depth to the paint. If you are *very* impatient, and want it to dry immediately, place greaseproof paper over the area and iron (as long as it's nowhere near a transfer).

Outlining

This is simply 'painting' lines to outline a motif or pattern, for example along feather shafts as on page 60, or round the separate leaves on the sweater on page 40. Squeeze the bottle firmly and evenly, moving along where you wish to go. Any breaks can be filled with a tiny blob.

Leave all plastic-look fabric paintwork to dry for at least 4 hours. It is washable within 48 hours. If you spill paint or paint yourself, wash it off quickly with soap and water; if it has dried on your skin, simply peel it off. Once dried on fabrics, though (as I know to my considerable cost), plastic-look fabric paints cannot be removed. Handwash the garment with care and never iron directly on to paint. These paints also withstand dry cleaning.

Dusting technique.

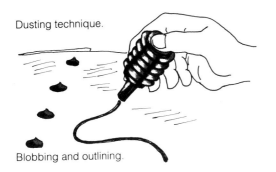

Blobbing and outlining.

Using Car-spray Paints

The paints that are used for cars are obtainable in super pearl and metallic finishes, and give wonderful effects when sprayed on to leather. Rigid feathers can be sprayed too, as can plastic trimmings such as buttons and pearl rope. One of the major benefits is that the paints dry very quickly.

However, when spraying, you must be careful. Try and do it outside (or in a very well ventilated room), and make sure you wear a mask (available from DIY shops). If doing a lot of spraying, drink milk to counteract the effects of the fumes.

Put the pieces of leather or the whole garment flat in a cardboard box, and spray. You can create great effects by mixing colours, and creasing up the leather. You could also make stencils and mask the leather in patterns. Do check the leather first – if the surface is too polished, the spray paint might not fix when dried.

Lace-effect on Leather

This is very easy and looks wonderful. Take a piece of leather, lie it flat in the box, and cover it with a larger piece of even-patterned lace. Stick the sides of the lace down on the cardboard with tape. Take two or three different colours of metallic car-spray paint and, starting with one, spray in swirls. With the second colour, repeat the pattern, but try not to cover the first. With the final colour, fill in the empty gaps, using the same free movement. When touch dry – approximately 5 minutes – remove lace and discard (it dries rigid, so it *could* be used on a hair or shoe clip).

Transfers

Transfers are made by screen-printing ink designs on to parchment paper. When the printing inks are heated as you iron the transfer in place on fabric, they melt and transfer the design to the fabric. There are many different varieties, a few of which I describe below, and have a look too at the list of suppliers on page 127. Transfers are best on cotton and cotton mix fabrics.

Some transfer papers come as a random design which can be cut up and scattered across the garment as desired. It is often nice to leave a small motif to place on a coordinating garment.

Standard Fusion Transfers

1. Try to use a flat rather than a steam iron: the holes in the latter could mean heat is not evenly distributed (although the rotation of the iron should ensure this). Set it to its highest setting.
2. Place the transfer(s), whether cut or whole, in the desired position(s) on the garment, design and ink side *down*.
3. Iron over the transfers, rotate *in sections* for 10 seconds, making sure all parts of the transfer are covered. To prevent scorching of more delicate fabrics, protect the areas around the transfer with sheets of greaseproof paper.
4. Leave to cool for 45 seconds. The inks solidify into the fabric, setting the transfer. (If you peel off impatiently beforehand, you will break the transfer.)
5. Peel off the parchment paper (and keep it if you intend foiling).

Foil Transfers

Some transfers are printed with inks that will take special foils, and these can look spectacular, adding yet another dimension. The design of the transfer is printed with two different kinds of ink, one which the foil sticks to when it melts, one which doesn't. There's no waste as these can be re-used again and again with amazing marbled results. The transfers and special foils shown in the book are available through mail order (see page 128).
1. Follow the process of standard fusion transfers above, and leave your iron at the hottest setting.

2. Cut out a piece of foil slightly larger than your transfer and place over it, *foil colour up*. Cover the whole thing with greaseproof paper.
3. Iron over the greaseproof paper covering the foil and transfer, rotating as above, for a quick 5 seconds.
4. Leave to cool for a good minute, then peel off the paper.

Marbled Foils

Always keep your used foils as they can be used *again* to create metallic marbled effects.
1. Place a used foil, colour side up, over your ironed-on transfer, cover with greaseproof paper, then iron and cool as before. The used, therefore incomplete, foil will have adhered to certain areas of the transfer only.
2. Place a new piece of foil in a different colour over the transfer, colour side up, cover with paper, and iron and cool as before. When the paper is removed, you will have created a fabulous multi-coloured effect.

Glitter Puff Transfers

These are transfers which puff out when ironed, giving a slightly three-dimensional look (see page 72). The small motifs are excellent on knits and other stretchy fabrics. It is best to use a small design or cut-up larger sheets of motifs and apply one motif at a time. For stockists, see page 127.
1. Heat the iron to its maximum temperature. Place the transfer in position in the same way as standard fusion transfers.
2. Press with the iron, rotating it as before, but for just a quick 8 seconds. Peel back the paper *immediately*, then leave to cool. (NB It is best to press and peel motif by motif).

Petal Holes

To make petal-shaped holes in leather, take the piece of leather in your non-working hand and push your index finger up from the underneath to the point where you want your petal hole. Take your scissors in your working hand and snip along the leather tip of your finger (figuratively speaking, of course), which will leave an oval petal shape. Practise on some scraps first, it's very easy.

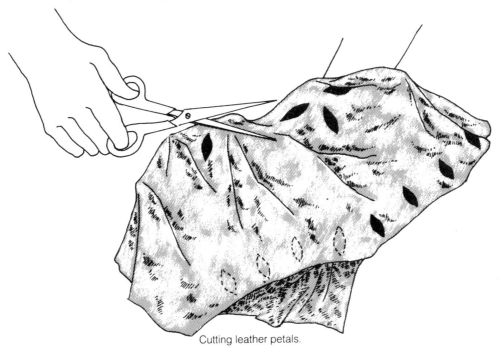

Cutting leather petals.

Tassels

These can be used as earrings (slot through a sleeper), and as decorations for anything from T-shirts to stockings. They can be bought ready-made at most haberdashery stores or you can make them yourself! They're so quick and easy, and because they can be made from almost any yarn you'll be able to match your colours up perfectly. Try mixing embroidery silk with crochet lurex or raffia with wool.

1. Cut a wide piece of cardboard to the desired depth of the tassel.

2. Place a piece of yarn across the top of the cardboard and then wind yarn round and round the cardboard until you get your desired fullness.

3. Tie the strands together firmly with a piece of yarn placed between card and yarn at the top of the cardboard, using an embroidery needle.

4. Remove the cardboard.

5. Cut through the strands at the base of the loop, keeping the tassel strands even.

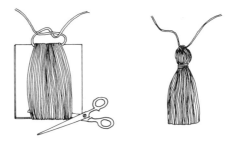

Making tassels.

Zip Roses

This is an original way of using boring zips! They are wonderfully decorative, and can be used as earrings and shoe clips as well. You can make two roses from one zip.

1. Take a metal-toothed zip of 55 cm (2 inches) in length, and remove the runner by snipping off the metal ends and sliding off. Discard. Separate in two by splitting the ends apart.

2. If gathering by machine, set the machine on the largest straight stitch and loosen the upper tension. Use a zipper foot and machine along the edge (not the metal tooth side). If doing by hand, make large tacking stitches along the same edge. Gather up loosely by knotting one end and gently pulling the thread at the other. Do not cut yet.

3. At one end, gather to make a rough circle of about 5 cm (2 inches) diameter (with the metal teeth on the outside), and pin in the desired position on the garment. Hand sew it in place, tucking and catching the raw edge underneath. Knot and cut off the sewing thread.

4. Take the other end of the zip, pull the tacking thread a little tighter, then curl it all around your fingers so that it falls into a rose shape. Twist this into the middle of the sewn circle, and hold in place with the non-sewing hand.

5. Then hand stitch the rose in place from underneath, making sure that every gather of the zip is caught. Give gentle tugs at the rose to check all parts are firmly in place. The stitching will probably not be even, due to the bulk of the zip, but don't worry as it is hidden. The important thing is that it stays on! (If making zip roses for accessories, sew the first circle on to something that will glue well on the earring clip or button – a scrap of leather for instance).

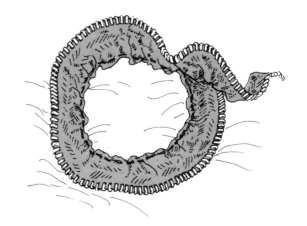

Making zip roses.

Fabric Flowers

Fabric flowers are easy to make out of offcuts or strips of colourful fabric. I used them to good effect on the yellow sweatshirt on page 57, where I edged them in silver lurex thread.

1. To make a rose, cut a strip of fabric approximately 5 cm (2 inches) wide and anything between 10–25 cm (4–10 inches) long.

2. Using a wide zig-zag and a long stitch, machine-sew some lurex thread along all sides of the strip, using transparent thread top and bottom.

3. Fold each strip in half and wind up to form an irregular rose shape.

4. Hand sew the rose together at the base with a couple of stitches to secure.

Polyester Flowers

Use polyester flowers for garment decoration as they do not fray or lose their shape or colour. Make sure their petals are attached to the stalk with a little plastic 'calyx' holder, and that they have plastic stems.

1. Take hold of the petals and gently pull away from the plastic holder and stem. You can then reassemble the flowers or mix layers from flowers of different colours to get an attractive design.

2. Position the flowers on clothes using either pins or a repositioning glue gun (see page 119). If you use the glue gun, you should push each petal firmly against the nozzle of the gun, then pull it off making sure that the glue comes off with it. You can then start trying the flowers on the garment, moving them from place to place until you are satisfied.

3. To attach small flowers securely, use claw diamantés or, if large, use the sew-on types (see page 116).

4. To prevent large petals from drooping, stud them in place at the ends. Arch them before studding to get a natural look.

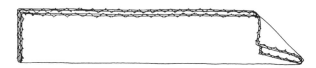

Making fabric roses.

Washing and Cleaning

Throughout the book I have indicated how specific garments should be cleaned or washed, but here are a few more general guidelines.

First of all, read the washing or cleaning label on the garment that you have decorated. Use that as your guide as to whether to clean or hand wash, taking into consideration the decorations you have applied.

Most garments are best washed inside out. Always wash in non-detergent products like Woolite (available from good chemists), and always wash *by hand*, in hand-hot water. A natural soap is excellent too, especially when rubbed on to stains. Never rub garments where the trimmings are, and do not leave anything to soak for too long, especially garments covered with sequins as the foil can flake off. Also, if Dylon products are not heat-sealed (ironed), the colours will wash out.

Do not spin or tumble dry. Gently squeeze out excess water, as you would when washing wool, pat with towels and dry flat, pulling into shape.

If the garment needs pressing, press gently around motifs. *Never* iron over transfer prints.

If in any doubt, dry clean a garment. Tell the cleaner to use Arklone which is indicated by the Ⓕ symbol. It does not dissolve glues and foils, and is generally gentler to clothes than other dry-cleaning solvents.

Summary of Washing Symbols

Symbol	Washing Temperature	
	Machine	Hand
1 / 95	very hot (95°C) to boil	hand hot 50°C or boil
2 / 60	hot 60°C	hand hot 50°C
3 / 60	hot 60°C	hand hot 50°C
4 / 50	hand hot 50°C	hand hot 50°C
5 / 40	warm 40°C	warm 40°C
6 / 40	warm 40°C	warm 40°C
7 / 40	warm 40°C	warm 40°C
8 / 30	cool 30°C	cool 30°C
🤚	HAND WASH ONLY	
⊠	DO NOT WASH	

△ Bleaching

When this symbol appears on a label household bleach must *not* be used.

◿ Ironing

The number of dots in the ironing symbol indicates the correct temperature setting – the fewer the dots the cooler the iron setting.

cool●   warm●●   hot●●●   do not iron ⊠

Dry Cleaning

The letter in the circle refers to the solvent which may be used in a dry cleaning process, and those using coin operated dry cleaning machines should check that the cleaning symbol shown on the label is the same as that in the instructions given on the front of the machine.

Ⓐ Goods normal for dry cleaning in all solvents.

Ⓟ Goods normal for dry cleaning in perchloroethylene, white spirit or Solvent 113 and Solvent 11.

Ⓕ Goods normal for dry cleaning in white spirit or Solvent 113.

◯ Do not dry clean.

Useful Stockists

You can buy leather by the skin from certain major department stores. Scraps of leather are available from shoemakers, some craft shops, and factories making leather goods. However, there is a wonderful shop in Islington, London N1, selling the most colourful assortment of leather, braids, old buttons, etc. The stock changes constantly so mail order is impossible.

Apostal's
106a Upper Street
Islington
London N1
Open Mon–Fri 10am–3.30pm
Saturday   10am–5pm

Pearce Tandy Leathercraft sell leather scraps by the bag, and also studs and diamantés. They have a mail order service. Send £1 (refundable with order) and you will receive a catalogue. Write to:

Pearce Tandy Leathercraft Ltd
Billing Park
Wellingborough Road
Northampton NN3 4BG
tel: (0604) 407177

Creative Beadcraft offer a comprehensive range of beads, diamantés, chains, studs and other small trimmings.

Creative Beadcraft Ltd
Mail Order: Shop:
Denmark Works   20 Princes Street
Sheepcote Dell Road   Hanover Square
Beamond End   London W1R 8PH
Nr Amersham
Bucks HP7 0RX
tel: (0494) 715606

For an exciting collection of new and old buttons and buckles, visit The Button Box.

The Button Box
44 Bedford Street
Covent Garden
London WC2E 9HA
tel: 01–240 2716

For a selection of transfer papers and foils, fabric paints, zip trimming, studs, diamantés, specialist equipment and a wide range of small trimmings, by *mail order only*, write to:

Jondean Ltd
105–107 Clarence Road
London E5 8EE

For a wide selection of beads, shells and jewellery findings (wholesale mail order available):

Hobby Horse
15–17 Langton Street
London SW10
tel: 01–351 6953

Obtaining Your Products

The products mentioned in *Fashion Magic* should easily be obtainable from the haberdashery department of large department stores, haberdashery shops, craft suppliers and art shops.

PAINTS
Plastic-look Fabric Paint: the trade names of the best-known makes are *Slick* and *Decopaint*. They come in different colours and finishes and also act as a 'glue'.
Dylon have a large range of fabric paints. These are purely decorative and will not act as an adhesive. They are widely available.

EQUIPMENT
Repositioning Glue Gun: the best make is the ATG 100 gun, which is manufactured by 3M and is obtainable from artists' suppliers and craft shops.
Leather Punch: available from haberdashery shops and craft shops.
Eyelet Punch: available from department stores.
Pattern-making Punch: available from haberdashery shops. If you experience any difficulty contact R. D. Franks, Kent House, Market Place, London W1   tel: 01–636 1244.
Studding Clamps: available from haberdashery shops and Creative Beadcraft Ltd.

STOP PRESS
There is a wonderful new gadget on the market, a bit like a staple gun, that attaches various sizes of studs and diamantés in seconds. It comes complete with easy-to-follow instructions. Details of stockists and mail order from: **Jondean Ltd**, 105–107 Clarence Road, London E5 8EE. (No personal callers)

If you have any problems obtaining materials featured in the book, fill in the form on page 128.

Reader Service

If you have any difficulty in obtaining any of the materials featured in *Fashion Magic*, fill in the form below, listing the products you are interested in. You will be sent details of your nearest retailer or a mail order supplier.

Garment decorating can be a lucrative business, which can be set up easily from home. But you need advanced decorating tools and know-how in order to be profitable. Seminars demonstrating these techniques, and information on how to set up your clothes decorating business are available. Complete and return the form below for further details.

Name .... Tel no ....

Address ....

.... Postcode ....

I would like to receive information on the following products:

....

....

....

....

....

I would like to set up a Garment Decorating Business from home. Please send me further details. ☐

I am a retailer and would like to stock the products. Please find my business card attached. ☐

Please send with a S.A.E. to:
Michelle Huberman,
P.O. Box 1717, London NW3 4RD.
Fax: 01–986 1420

If you do not wish to remove this page, please copy on to a separate sheet of paper.